John Carroll Randolph

Patriotic Songs

For school and home

John Carroll Randolph

Patriotic Songs
For school and home

ISBN/EAN: 9783337309459

Printed in Europe, USA, Canada, Australia, Japan

Cover: Foto ©Thomas Meinert / pixelio.de

More available books at **www.hansebooks.com**

PATRIOTIC SONGS

FOR

SCHOOL AND HOME

SELECTED AND ARRANGED BY

JOHN CARROLL RANDOLPH

BOSTON

OLIVER DITSON COMPANY

NEW YORK   PHILADELPHIA   CHICAGO
C. H. DITSON & CO.   J. E. DITSON & CO.   LYON & HEALY

PREFACE.

The past decade has been marked by a deepening and quickening of the national conscious-ness. Nowhere has this growth so revealed itself as in the common schools, where patriotic themes and occasions, and the study of American history receive a degree of attention never before known. Recent events in our national life have served to intensify this trend, and deeply stir the spirit of patriotism. This spirit, in turn, has found expression in new and stirring music, and has brought into renewed favor melodies of earlier days. This volume has been prepared in response to a demand for a comprehensive collection of music, old and new, devoted exclusively to the theme of Country and Home, and arranged for school use. The subdivisions of the book, as indicated in its arrangement, and recorded in the Table of Contents, show the scope of the work.

Two features distinguish the volume:

First, its plan and size. The volume is devoted entirely to Patriotic music, and it is be-lieved that no such work of this character has thus far appeared in print. As the love of home is the natural basis of love of country, a few songs of home have been included. Music and words that are sectional in character have been carefully omitted, and it is believed that the vol-ume in its entirety will be found in perfect consonance with the spirit of concord so happily man-ifest in our land.

Second, The unique arrangement of the voice parts has been made in response to the urgent demand of experienced workers in the public schools. As the tenor part, to be sung at all, must in most cases be sung — in schools — by an alto voice (boy or girl), this part has throughout the book been written in the G clef, and denominated Alto-Tenor. This is a duplication of the orig-inal tenor part, which will be found in its usual place on the bass staff.

The alto part has been written beneath the soprano or treble, as a second soprano.

Wherever needed, the music has been transposed into keys that will accommodate young voices, by avoiding high notes in the soprano part, and, on the other hand, low notes in the bass part. The range of the latter has also been restricted wherever possible.

While the majority of the choruses are in four-part harmony, a number of three-part songs prepared for the collection have been included.

That the work may meet the demand that called it forth is the wish of the compiler.

JOHN CARROLL RANDOLPH.

Boston, November, 1898.

CONTENTS.

OUR COUNTRY.

OUR HEROES.

(*MEMORIAL DAY.*)

OUR HOMES.

HYMNS OF PATRIOTISM.

NATIONAL DAYS.

MISCELLANEOUS.

OUR COUNTRY

MY COUNTRY, 'TIS OF THEE.

AMERICA.

First sung in Park Street Church, Boston, July 4, 1832.

SAMUEL FRANCIS SMITH (1808–1895.)   Author of music unknown.

1st AND 2d SOPRANO.

1. My coun-try, 'tis of thee, Sweet land of lib - er - ty, Of thee I sing; Land where my
2. My na - tive coun - try, thee, Land of the no - ble free, Thy name I love; I love thy
3. Let mu - sic swell the breeze, And ring from all the trees Sweet Freedom's song; Let mor - tal
4. Our fa-thers' God! to Thee, Au - thor of lib - er - ty, To Thee we sing: Long may our

ALTO-TENOR.

1. My coun-try, 'tis of thee, Sweet land of lib - er - ty, Of thee I sing; Land where my
2. My na - tive coun - try, thee, Land of the no - ble free, Thy name I love; I love thy
3. Let mu - sic swell the breeze, And ring from all the trees, Sweet Freedom's song; Let mor - tal
4. Our fa-thers' God! to Thee, Au - thor of lib - er - ty, To Thee we sing: Long may our

TENOR AND BASS.

fa - thers died, Land of the Pilgrim's pride, From ev - 'ry moun-tain side Let free - dom ring.
rocks and rills, Thy woods and tem - pled hills; My heart with rap -ture thrills, Like that a - bove.
tongues a - wake, Let all that breathe partake, Let rocks their si - lence break, The sound pro-long.
land be brightWith free-dom's ho - ly light, Pro - tect us by Thy might, Great God, our King.

fa - thers died, Land of the Pilgrim's pride, From ev - 'ry moun-tain side Let free - dom ring.
rocks and rills, Thy woods and tem - pled hills; My heart with rap -ture thrills, Like that a - bove.
tongues a - wake, Let all that breathe partake, Let rocks their si - lence break, The sound pro-long.
land be brightWith free-dom's ho - ly light, Pro - tect us by Thy might, Great God, our King.

COLUMBIA, THE GEM OF THE OCEAN.

THE RED, WHITE, AND BLUE.

Words and Music by DAVID T. SHAW.

1. O Co-lum-bia! the gem of the o-cean, The home of the brave and the
2. When war winged its wide des-o-la-tion, And threatened the land to de-
3. "Old Glo-ry" to greet, now come hith-er, With eyes full of love to the

free, . The shrine of each pa-triot's de-vo-tion, A
form, . The ark then of free-dom's foun-da-tion, Co-
brim; . May the wreaths of our he-roes ne'er with-er, Nor a

world of-fers hom-age to thee. Thy man-dates make he-roes as-
lum-bia, rode safe thro' the storm; With her gar-lands of vic-t'ry a-
star of our ban-ner grow dim; May the ser-vice u-nit-ed ne'er

sem-ble, When Lib-er-ty's form stands in view; Thy
round her, When so proud-ly she bore her brave crew, With her
sev-er, But they to our col-ors prove true! The

flag proudly float-ing be - fore her, Three cheers for the Red, White, and Blue.
Ar - my and Na - vy for ev - er, Three cheers for the Red, White, and Blue.

f

CHORUS.
1ST AND 2D SOPRANO

Three cheers for the Red, White, and Blue, Three cheers for the Red, White, and
Three cheers for the Red, White, and Blue, Three cheers for the Red, White, and
Three cheers for the Red, White, and Blue, Three cheers for the Red, White, and

ALTO-TENOR.

Three cheers for the Red, White, and Blue, White and Blue, Three cheers for the Red, White, and
Three cheers for the Red, White, and Blue, White and Blue, Three cheers for the Red, White, and
Three cheers for the Red, White, and Blue, White and Blue, Three cheers for the Red, White, and

TENOR AND BASS.

f

ff

Blue, Thy ban-ners make ty-ian - ny tremble, Three cheers for the Red, White, and Blue.
Blue, With her flag proudly float-ing be -fore her, Three cheers for the Red, White, and Blue.
Blue, The Ar-my and Na -vy for ev-er, Three cheers for the Red, White, and Blue.

ff

Blue, White and Blue, Thy banners make tyran-ny tremble, Three cheers for the Red, White, and Blue.
Blue, White and Blue, With her flag proudly floating before her, Three cheers for the Red, White, and Blue.
Blue, White and Blue, The Army and Na - vy for ev-er, Three cheers for the Red, White, and Blue.

ff

DIXIE'S LAND.

Dan. D. Emmett. Arr. by F. M.

1. I wish I was in de land ob cot-ton, Old times dar am not for-got-ten, Look a-way! Look a-way! Look a-way! Dix-ie Land! In Dix-ie Land whar I was born in Ear-ly in one fros-ty morn-in', Look a-way! Look a-way! Look a-way! Dix-ie Land!

2. Old Mis-sus mar-ry "Will-de-weab-er," Wil-lium was a gay de-ceab-er, Look a-way! Look a-way! Look a-way! Dix-ie Land! But when he put his arm a-round 'er He smil'd as fierce as a for-ty pound-er, Look a-way! Look a-way! Look a-way! Dix-ie Land!

3. His face was sharp as a butch-er's cleab-er, But dat did not seem to greab 'er, Look a-way! Look a-way! Look a-way! Dix-ie Land! Old Mis-sus act-ed de fool-ish part, And died for a man dat broke her heart, Look a-way! Look a-way! Look a-way! Dix-ie Land!

4. Now here's a health to the next old Mis-sus, An' all de gals dat want to kiss us, Look a-way! Look a-way! Look a-way! Dix-ie Land! But if you want to drive 'way sor-row Come an' hear dis song to-mor-row, Look a-way! Look a-way! Look a-way! Dix-ie Land!

5. Dar's buckwheat cakes an' In-jun bat-ter Makes you fat or a lit-tle fat-ter, Look a-way! Look a-way! Look a-way! Dix-ie Land! Den hoe it down an' scratch your grab-ble, To Dix-ie's land I'm bound to trab-ble, Look a-way! Look a-way! Look a-way! Dix-ie Land!

CHORUS.
1ST AND 2D SOPRANO.

Den I wish I was in Dix - ie, Hoo - ray! Hoo - ray! In Dix - ie Land I'll

ALTO-TENOR.

Den I wish I was in Dix - ie, Hoo - ray! Hoo - ray! In Dix - ie Land I'll

TENOR AND BASS.

Den I wish I was in Dix - ie, Hoo - ray! Hoo - ray! In Dix - ie Land I'll

took my stand, To lib an' die in Dix - ie, A - way, A - way, A -

took my stand, To lib an' die in Dix - ie, A - way, A - way, A -

took my stand, To lib an' die in Dix - ie, A - way, A - way, A -

D.S.

way down south in Dix - ie, A - way, A - way, A - way down south in Dix - ie.

way down south in Dix - ie, A - way, A - way, A - way down south in Dix - ie.

down south in Dix - ie, A - way, A - way, A - way down south in Dix - ie.

D.S.

WM. B. BRADBURY.

1. Firm - ly stand,   Firm - ly stand,   My na - tive land!   Firm - ly
2. Safe - ly dwell,   Safe - ly dwell,   My na - tive land!   Safe - ly
3. Sing for joy,   Sing for joy,   My na - tive land!   Sing for

ALTO—TENOR.

1. Firm - ly stand,   Firm - ly stand,   My na - tive land!
2. Safe - ly dwell,   Safe - ly dwell,   My na - tive land!
3. Sing for joy,   Sing for joy,   My na - tive land!

TENOR AND BASS.

Firm - ly stand, ... Firm - ly stand, My na - tive land! Firm - ly
Safe - ly dwell, ... Safe - ly dwell, My na - tive land! Safe - ly
Sing for joy, ... Sing for joy, My na - tive land! Sing for

Firm - ly
Safe - ly
Sing for

stand,   Firm - ly stand,   My na - tive land!   Na - tive land!
dwell,   Safe - ly dwell,   My na - tive land!   Na - tive land!
joy,   Sing for joy,   My na - tive land!   Na - tive land!

Firm - ly stand,   My na - tive land!   Na - tive land!
Safe - ly dwell,   My na - tive land!   Na - tive land!
Sing for joy,   My na - tive land!   Na - tive land!

stand, Firm - ly stand,   My na - tive land!   na - tive land!
dwell, Safe - ly dwell,   My na - tive land!   na - tive land!
joy, Sing for joy,   My na - tive land!   na - tive land!

May thy sons u - ni - ted stand, Firm and true for ev - er! God for - bid the
In thee dwells a no - ble band, All thy need to cher - ish! God with might will

True in heart and true in hand, All that's love - ly cher - ish! Thus shall God re -
May thy sons u - ni - ted stand, Firm and true for ev - er! God for - bid the
In thee dwells a no - ble band, All thy need to cher - ish! God with might will

True in heart and true in hand, All that's love - ly cher - ish! Thus shall God re -
May thy sons u - ni - ted stand, Firm and true for ev - er! God for - bid the
In thee dwells a no - ble band, All thy need to cher - ish! God with might will

Free - dom, Free - dom,

main thy friend, Thus shall heav'n thy walls de - fend, Free - dom, Free - dom,
day should rise, When 'tis said our Free - dom dies, Free - dom, Free - dom,
guard thee round, While thy steps in truth are bound, Free - dom, Free - dom,

main thy friend, Thus shall heav'n thy walls de - fend, Free - dom, Free - dom,
day should rise, When 'tis said our Free - dom dies, Free - dom, Free - dom,
guard thee round, While thy steps in truth are bound, Free - dom, Free - dom,

main thy friend, Thus shall heav'n thy walls de - fend, Free - dom, Free - dom,
day should rise, When 'tis said our Free - dom dies, Free - dom, Free - dom,
guard thee round While thy steps in truth are bound, Free - dom, Free - dom,

Free-dom shall not per-ish, Free-dom, Free - dom, Free - dom, Free-dom shall not
Free-dom shall not per-ish, Free - - dom, Free-dom, Free-dom shall not
Free-dom shall not per-ish, Free-dom, Free-dom, Free-dom shall not
Firm - ly stand, Firm - ly
ff
per - ish! Firm - ly stand, ... Firm - ly
per - ish! Firm - ly stand, Firm - ly stand, Firm - ly
per - ish! Firm - ly, Firm - ly stand, Firm - ly, Firm - ly stand, Firm - ly, Firm - ly
stand, ... My na - tive land, my na - tive land, my na - tive land!
stand, My na - tive land, my na - - - - - tive land!
stand, My na - tive land, my na - - - - tive land!
stand, My na - tive land, my na - tive, na - - - tive land!
Ped. *

FIRMLY STAND, O NATIVE LAND.

HANS G. NÄGELI (1773-1836.)
Arr. by GEO. F. WILSON.

1. Firm - ly stand, firm - ly stand, O na - tive land! Firm - ly stand, firm - ly
2. True re - main, true re - main, O na - tive land! True re - main, true re -
3. Be a - wake, be a - wake, O na - tive land! Be a - wake, be a -

stand, O na - tive land! True in heart, and strong of hand, Hold the right un-
main, O na - tive land! Nev - er weak in free-dom's band, True to du - ty
wake, O na - tive land! Soul to soul, we take our stand, La - ter tri - umph

bend - ing; Sword of jus - tice thou shalt wield, Truth and hon - or as thy shield,
ev - er, Mind - ful of the fa - thers brave Who their lives for coun - try gave,
bring - ing, May the throb of ev - 'ry heart, Wis - dom to our song im - part,

Free - dom's, Free - dom's, Free - dom's cause de - fend - ing. Firm - ly stand, firm - ly
Dy - ing, dy - ing, that it ne'er may sev - er. True re - main, true re -
Ring - ing, ring - ing, still for free - dom ring - ing. Be a - wake, be a -

stand, firm - ly stand, firm - ly stand, O na - tive land, My own dear na - tive land!
main, true re - main, true re - main, O na - tive land, My own dear na - tive land!
wake, be a - wake, be a - wake, O na - tive land, My own dear na - tive land!

FREEDOM'S LAND—AMERICA.

Gen. LUTHER STEPHENSON.

Air "O Tannenbaum."

1ST AND 2D SOPRANO.

1. Come, free-men, join in joy - ful song, Hap - py Land! A - mer - i - ca! With
2. In dis - tant climes where none are free, Freedom's Land! A - mer - i - ca! And
3. Thy hills and loft - y moun-tain peaks, Glo - rious Land! A - mer - i - ca! And
4. O God, in grate - ful praise we sing, Still guard our land! A - mer - i - ca! And

ALTO-TENOR.

1. Come, free-men, join in joy - ful song, Hap - py Land! A - mer - i - ca! With
2. In dis - tant climes where none are free, Free-dom's Land! A - mer - i - ca! And
3. Thy hills and loft - y moun-tain peaks, Glo - rious Land! A - mer - i - ca! And
4. O God, in grate - ful praise we sing, Still guard our land! A - mer - i - ca! And

TENOR AND BASS.

1. Come, free - men, join in joy - ful song, Hap - py Land! A - mer - i - ca! With
2. In dis - tant climes where none are free, Free-dom's Land! A - mer - i - ca! And
3. Thy hills and loft - y moun-tain peaks, Glo - rious Land! A - mer - i - ca! And
4. O God, in grate - ful praise we sing, Still guard our land! A - mer - i - ca! And

heart and voice the strain pro - long, Hap - py Land! A - mer - i - ca! Where
long - ing eyes are turned to thee, Free-dom's Land! A - mer - i - ca! With
rush - ing streams with gran - deur speak; Glo - rious Land! A - mer - i - ca! The
hum - ble hearts to Thee we bring; Still guard our Land! A - mer - i - ca! O

heart and voice the strain pro - long, Hap - py Land! A - mer - i - ca! Where
long - ing eyes are turned to thee, Free-dom's Land! A - mer - i - ca! With
rush - ing streams with gran - deur speak; Glo - rious Land! A - mer - i - ca! The
hum - ble hearts to Thee we bring; Still guard our Land! A - mer - i - ca! O

heart and voice the strain pro - long, Hap - py Land! A - mer - i - ca! Where
long - ing eyes are turned to thee, Free - dom's Land! A - mer - i - ca! With
rush - ing streams with gran - deur speak; Glo - rious Land! A - mer - i - ca! The
hum - ble hearts to Thee we bring; Still guard our land! A - mer - i - ca! O

hope and love and vir-tue reign, And hap-py homes their joys pro-claim, While
Lib-er-ty a bea-con light, A star of Hope in sor-row's night, With
fer-tile fields and for-ests grand, From lake to sea, the Gold-en Land! The
keep us true, and make us free, Our coun-try great and wor-thy Thee, The

hope and love and vir-tue reign, And hap-py homes their joys pro-claim, While
Lib-er-ty a bea-con light, A star of Hope in sor-row's night, With
fer-tile fields and for-ests grand, From lake to sea, the Gold-en Land! The
keep us true, and make us free, Our coun-try great and wor-thy Thee, The

hope and love and vir-tue reign, And hap-py homes their joys pro-claim, While
Lib-er-ty a bea-con light, A star of hope in sor-row's night, With
fer-tile fields and for-ests grand, From lake to sea, the Gold-en Land! The
keep us true, and make us free, Our coun-try great and wor-thy Thee, The

chil-dren bless thy hon-ored name; Hap-py Land! A-mer-i-ca!
e-qual laws and e-qual rights; Free-dom's Land! A-mer-i-ca!
ice-bound coast, the south-ern strand; Glo-rious Land! A-mer-i-ca!
glo-rious home of lib-er-ty; O bless our land, A-mer-i-ca!

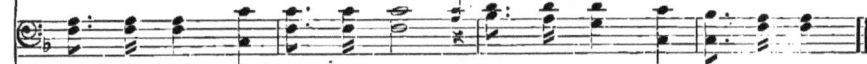

chil-dren bless thy hon-ored name; Hap-py Land! A-mer-i-ca!
e-qual laws and e-qual rights; Free-dom's Land! A-mer-i-ca!
ice-bound coast, the south-ern strand; Glo-rious Land! A-mer-i-ca!
glo-rious home of lib-er-ty; O bless our land, A-mer-i-ca!

chil-dren bless thy hon-ored name; Hap-py Land! A-mer-i-ca!
e-qual laws and e-qual rights; Free-dom's Land! A-mer-i-ca!
ice-bound coast, the south-ern strand; Glo-rious Land! A-mer-i-ca!
glo-rious home of lib-er-ty; O bless our land, A-mer-i-ca!

HAIL COLUMBIA!

Origin of Hail Columbia. — This popular National Song was written in 1798 by Judge Hopkinson. At that period a war with France was thought inevitable. Party-spirit ran high among all classes. A theatre was open in Philadelphia, and a young man who had some talent as a singer announced his benefit on its boards. He was acquainted with Judge Hopkinson and, discouraged at his prospect of success, called on him on Saturday afternoon and stated that he feared a loss instead of a benefit, but that if he could get a patriotic song adapted to the tune of "The President's March," then quite popular, he might depend on a full house. The Judge replied that he would try to furnish one. The next afternoon the young man came again, and the song was handed him. It was announced on Monday morning. In the evening the theatre was crowded to excess, and continued to be night after night through the entire season — the song being loudly encored and repeated many times during each night, the audience joining in the chorus. It was sung at night in the streets by large assemblies of citizens, including Members of Congress, and found favor with both parties, as neither could disavow its sentiments.

JOSEPH HOPKINSON,
1770–1842.

Arr. from "The President's March," by PROFESSOR PHYLA.
which was first played when Washington came to New York to be
inaugurated in 1789.

1. Hail! Co-lum-bia, hap-py land! Hail! ye he-roes, heav'n-born band, Who
2. Im-mor-tal Pa-triots, rise once more! De-fend your rights, de-fend your shore: Let
3. Sound, sound the trump of fame! Let Wash-ing-ton's great name Ring
4. Be-hold the chief who now com-mands, Once more to serve his coun-try, stands The

fought and bled in free - dom's cause, Who fought and bled in free - dom's cause, And
no rude foe, with im - pious hand, Let no rude foe, with im - pious hand, In-
through the world with loud ap - plause! Ring through the world with loud ap - plause! Let
rock on which the storm will beat, The rock on which the storm will beat! But

when the storm of war was gone, En - joyed the peace your
vade the shrine where sa - cred lies Of toil and blood the
ev - 'ry clime to free - dom dear, Lis - ten with a
armed in vir - tue, firm and true, His hopes are fixed on

val - or won; Let in - de - pen - dence be your boast,
well earn'd prize; While of - f'ring peace, sin - cere and just, In
joy - ful ear; With e - qual skill, with stead - y pow'r, He
heav'n and you; When hope was sink - ing in dis - may, When

Ev - er mind - ful what it cost, Ev - er grate - ful
heav'n we place a man - ly trust, That truth and jus - tice
gov - erns in the fear - ful hour Of hor - rid war, or
gloom ob - scured Co - lum - bia's day, His stead - y mind, from

for the prize, Let its al - tar reach the skies.
may pre - vail, And ev - 'ry scheme of bond - age fall!
guides with ease The hap - pier time of hon - est peace.
chang - es free, Re - solved on death or lib - er - ty.
Chorus.
1st and 2d Soprano.
f
Firm, u - ni - ted let us be, Rally - ing round our lib - er - ty,
Alto-Tenor.
f
Firm, u - ni - ted let us be, Rally - ing round our lib - er - ty,
Tenor and Bass.
f
Firm, u - ni - ted let us be, Rally - ing round our lib - er - ty,
f
As a band of broth - ers joined, Peace and safe - ty we shall find.
3
3
As a band of broth - ers joined, Peace and safe - ty we shall find.
As a band of broth - ers joined, Peace and safe - ty we shall find.
3
3

HAIL! GLORIOUS LAND OF LOVE AND PEACE.

John Treanor.
Maestoso.
Soprano and Alto.

A. Tregina.
Arr. by F. E. Chapman.

Bass.

Hail! Glorious Land of Love and Peace! Fruit - ful Home of Truth and Freedom! Whose

sky - kiss'd mountains, vales, and in - land seas Are guard - ed for aye by O - - cean.

Hail! Land of Gifts, in thee shall be found Hu - man - i - ty's pro - gress, e - volv'd from all

sta - tions. Free Con - science is thine; free Al - tars a - bound To the glo - ry of

Him who is Lord God of Na - tions. Hail! Fair Co - lum - bla! Bright Star of the
Hail! Fair Co - lum - bla! Bright

West! Hope of Hu - man - i - ty! Home of the Free! Cham - pion of

Star of the West! Hope of Hu - man - i - ty! Home of the Free! Champion of

Jus - tice! Im - mor - tal and blest! These, now and for ev - er, thy ti - tles shall be.

W. P. Chamberlain.
Arr. by A. W.

1. This is our own, our na-tive home, Tho' poor and rough she be,
2. Shall not the land, tho' poor she be, That gave a Web-ster
3. They tell us of our freez-ing clime, Our hard and rug-ged
4. Oth-ers may seek the west-ern clime; They say 'tis pass-ing

be, The home of man-y a no-ble soul, The birth-place of the
birth, With pride step forth to take her place With the might-iest of the
soil, Which hard-ly half re-pays us for Our spring-time care and
fair, That sun-ny are its laugh-ing skies And soft its balm-y

free. We'll love her rocks and riv-ers, Till death our quick-blood stills; Hur-
earth? Then for his sake, whose lofty fame Our far-thest bound'ries fills, We'll
toil. Yet gai-ly sings the merry boy As the home-stead farm he tills; Hur-
air. We'll lin-ger round our childhood's home, Till age our warm blood chills, Till we

rah for old New Eng-land! And her cloud-capped gran-ite hills.
shout for old New Eng-land! And her cloud-capped gran-ite hills.
rah for old New Eng-land! And her cloud-capped gran-ite hills.
die in old New Eng-land! And sleep be-neath her hills.

1ST AND 2D SOPRANO.

Hur - rah   for old New Eng-land!   And her cloud-capped gran - ite hills,   Hur -

ALTO–TENOR.

Hur - rah   for old New Eng-land!   And her cloud-capped gran - ite hills,   Hur -

TENOR AND BASS.

Hur - rah   for old New Eng-land!   And her cloud-capped gran - ite hills,   Hur -

rah   for old New Eng - land!   And her cloud - capped gran - ite hills.

rah   for old New Eng - land!   And her cloud - capped gran - ite hills.

rah   for old New Eng - land!   And her cloud - capped gran - ite hills.

LAND OF GREATNESS! HOME OF GLORY!

AUSTRIAN NATIONAL HYMN.

A. J. Foxwell.

Franz Joseph Haydn (1732-1809.)

1st and 2d Soprano.

1. Land of great-ness! Home of glo - ry! Might - y birth-place of the free!
2. No - ble deeds of old in - spir - ing Ev - 'ry heart with lof - ty aim,
3. Homes by safe de - fence sur - round - ed, Rights which make our free - dom sure,

Alto—Tenor.

1. Land of great-ness! Home of glo - ry! Might - y birth-place of the free!
2. No - ble deeds of old in - spir - ing Ev - 'ry heart with lof - ty aim,
3. Homes by safe de - fence sur - round - ed, Rights which make our free - dom sure,

Tenor and Bass.

1. Land of great-ness! Home of glo - ry! Might - y birth-place of the free!
2. No - ble deeds of old in - spir - ing Ev - 'ry heart with lof - ty aim,
3. Homes by safe de - fence sur - round - ed, Rights which make our free - dom sure,

Famed a - like in song and sto - ry! All thy sons shall hon - or thee.
Now our em - u - la - tion fir - ing, Lead us on to great - er fame.
Laws on e - qual jus - tice found - ed, These will loy - al - ty se - cure.

Famed a - like in song and sto - ry! All thy sons shall hon - or thee.
Now our em - u - la - tion fir - ing, Lead us on to great - er fame.
Laws on e - qual jus - tice found - ed, These will loy - al - ty se - cure.

Famed a - like in song and sto - ry! All thy sons shall hon - or thee.
Now our em - u - la - tion fir - ing, Lead us on to great - er fame.
Laws on e - qual jus - tice found - ed, These will loy - al - ty se - cure.

North and South are firm - ly band - ed, East and West as one u - nite;
So shall love and truth un - shak - en, Stur - dy cour - age, hon - est worth,
While with love and zeal un - ceas - ing, We are join - ing heart and hand,

North and South are firm - ly band - ed, East and West as one u - nite;
So shall love and truth un - shak - en, Stur - dy cour - age, hon - est worth,
While with love and zeal un - ceas - ing, We are join - ing heart and hand,

North and South are firm - ly band - ed, East and West as one u - nite;
So shall love and truth un - shak - en, Stur - dy cour - age, hon - est worth,
While with love and zeal un - ceas - ing, We are join - ing heart and hand,

All by hon - or well com-mand - ed, Strong in striv - ing for the right.
Might - y ech - oes still a - wak - en, To the far - thest bounds of earth.
Shine, in bright - ness yet in - creas - ing, Shine, O dear - est Fa - ther - land.

All by hon - or well com-mand - ed, Strong in striv - ing for the right.
Might - y ech - oes still a - wak - en, To the far - thest bounds of earth.
Shine, in bright - ness yet in - creas - ing, Shine, O dear - est Fa - ther - land.

All by hon - or well com-mand - ed, Strong in striv - ing for the right.
Might - y ech - oes still a - wak - en, To the far - thest bounds of earth.
Shine, in bright - ness yet in - creas - ing, Shine, O dear - est Fa - ther - land.

Air, "O Tannenbaum."
German Folk-song, (1799).

1ST AND 2D SOPRANO.

1. Thou wilt not cow - er in the dust, Ma - ry - land! my Ma - ry - land!
2. I see no blush up - on thy cheek, Ma - ry - land! my Ma - ry - land!
3. I hear the dis - tant thun - der hum, Ma - ry - land! my Ma - ry - land!

ALTO-TENOR.

1. Thou wilt not cow - er in the dust, Ma - ry - land! my Ma - ry - land!
2. I see no blush up - on thy cheek, Ma - ry - land! my Ma - ry - land!
3. I hear the dis - tant thun - der hum, Ma - ry - land! my Ma - ry - land!

TENOR AND BASS.

1. Thou wilt not cow - er in the dust, Ma - ry - land! my Ma - ry - land!
2. I see no blush up - on thy cheek, Ma - ry - land! my Ma - ry - land!
3. I hear the dis - tant thun - der hum, Ma - ry - land! my Ma - ry - land!

Thy beam - ing sword shall nev - er rust, Ma - ry - land! my Ma - ry - land!
Tho' thou wast ev - er brave - ly meek, Ma - ry - land! my Ma - ry - land!
The Old Line bu - gle, fife, and drum, Ma - ry - land! my Ma - ry - land!

Thy beam - ing sword shall nev - er rust, Ma - ry - land! my Ma - ry - land!
Tho' thou wast ev - er brave - ly meek, Ma - ry - land! my Ma - ry - land!
The Old Line bu - gle, fife, and drum, Ma - ry - land! my Ma - ry - land!

Thy beam - ing sword shall nev - er rust, Ma - ry - land! my Ma - ry - land!
Tho' thou wast ev - er brave - ly meek, Ma - ry - land! my Ma - ry - land!
The Old Line bu - gle, fife, and drum, Ma - ry - land! my Ma - ry - land!

Re - mem - ber Car - roll's sa - cred trust, Re - mem - ber How - ard's
For life and death, for woe and weal, Thy peer - less chiv - al -
Come! to thine own he - ro - ic throng, That stalks with lib - er -

Re - mem - ber Car - roll's sa - cred trust, Re - mem - ber How - ard's
For life and death, for woe and weal, Thy peer - less chiv - al -
Come! to thine own he - ro - ic throng, That stalks with lib - er -

Re - mem - ber Car - roll's sa - cred trust, Re - mem - ber How - ard's
For life and death, for woe and weal, Thy peer - less chiv - al -
Come! to thine own he - ro - ic throng, That stalks with lib - er -

war - like thrust, And all thy slum - b'rers with the just, Ma - ry - land! my Ma - ry - land!
ry re - veal, And gird thy beau - teous limbs with steel, Ma - ry - land! my Ma - ry - land!
ty a - long, And ring thy daunt - less slo - gan song, Ma - ry - land! my Ma - ry - land!

war - like thrust, And all thy slum - b'rers with the just, Ma - ry - land! my Ma - ry - land!
ry re - veal, And gird thy beau - teous limbs with steel, Ma - ry - land! my Ma - ry - land!
ty a - long, And ring thy daunt - less slo - gan song, Ma - ry - land! my Ma - ry - land!

war - like thrust, And all thy slum - b'rers with the just, Ma - ry - land! my Ma - ry - land!
ry re - veal, And gird thy beau - teous limbs with steel, Ma - ry - land! my Ma - ry - land!
ty a - long, And ring thy daunt - less slo - gan song, Ma - ry - land! my Ma - ry - land!

NATIVE LAND, UNITED LAND.

J. C. MACY.
1ST AND 2D SOPRANO.

Air: "O Tannenbaum."
German Folk-song, (1799).

ALTO-TENOR.

1. A song of praise we sing for thee, Na - tive land, U - ni - ted land.
2. Our fa - thers' deeds we cher - ish still, Pa - triot land, U - ni - ted land.
3. But not by con - quest do we thrive, Na - tive land, U - ni - ted land.

TENOR AND BASS.

1. A song of praise we sing for thee, Na - tive land, U - ni - ted land.
2. Our fa - thers' deeds we cher - ish still, Pa - triot land, U - ni - ted land.
3. But not by con - quest do we thrive, Na - tive land, U - ni - ted land.

1. A song of praise we sing for thee, Na - tive land, U - ni - ted land.
2. Our fa - thers' deeds we cher - ish still, Pa - triot land, U - ni - ted land.
3. But not by con - quest do we thrive, Na - tive land, U - ni - ted land.

Thy heart beats true, thy sons are true, Na - tive land, dear na - tive land.
With rev - 'rence we main - tain their will, Pil - grim's land, be - lov - ed land.
For God and hu - man rights we strive, Fa - vor'd land, O heav'n-blest land.

Thy heart beats true, thy sons are true, Na - tive land, dear na - tive land.
With rev - 'rence we main - tain their will, Pil - grim's land, be - lov - ed land.
For God and hu - man rights we strive, Fa - vor'd land, O heav'n-blest land.

Thy heart beats true, thy sons are true, Na - tive land, dear na - tive land.
With rev - 'rence we main - tain their will, Pil - grim's land, be - lov - ed land.
For God and hu - man rights we strive, Fa - vor'd land, O heav'n-blest land.

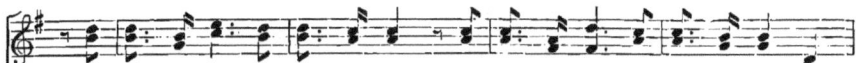

Thy chil - dren rise when thou dost call, And treach-'rous foes be - fore thee fall! The
The world has learned our pow'r and might, When wrong would seek to crush the right; We
Our ben - e - fits to all are free, Our deeds are for hu - man - i - ty; And

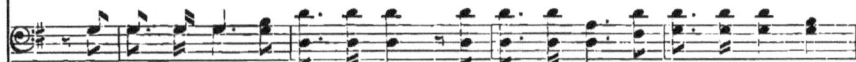

Thy chil - dren rise when thou dost call, And treach-'rous foes be - fore thee fall! The
The world has learned our pow'r and might, When wrong would seek to crush the right; We
Our ben - e - fits to all are free, Our deeds are for hu - man - i - ty; And

Thy chil - dren rise when thou dost call, And treach-'rous foes · be - fore thee fall! The
The world has learned our pow'r and might, When wrong would seek to crush the right; We
Our ben - e - fits to all are free, Our deeds are for hu - man - i - ty; And

na - tion's flag still waves o'er all! Free-dom's land, O Free - dom's land!
shed a - broad Truth's glo - rious light, Free-dom's land, be - lov - ed land.
may we thus for ev - er be, Na - tive land, U - nit - ed land.

na - tion's flag still waves o'er all! Free-dom's land! O Free - dom's land!
shed a - broad Truth's glo - rious light, Free-dom's land, be - lov - ed land.
may we thus for ev - er be, Na - tive land, U - nit - ed land.

na - tion's flag still waves o'er all! . Free-dom's land, O Free - dom's land!
shed a - broad Truth's glo - rious light, Free-dom's land, be - lov - ed land.
may we thus for ev - er be, Na - tive land, U - nit - ed land.

NEW ENGLAND, NEW ENGLAND.

I. T. Stoddard.

Andante.

1. New Eng-land, New Eng-land, my home o'er the sea, My heart as I
2. Thy breez-es are health-ful, and clear are thy rills, And the har-vest waves
3. There's home in New Eng-land, where dear ones of mine , Are think-ing of

1. New Eng-land, New Eng-land, my home o'er the sea, My heart as I
2. Thy breez-es are health-ful, and clear are thy rills, And the har-vest waves
3. There's home in New Eng-land, where dear ones of mine Are think-ing of

1. New Eng-land, New Eng-land, my home o'er the sea, My heart as I
2. Thy breez-es are health-ful, and clear are thy rills, And the har-vest waves
3. There's home in New Eng-land, where dear ones of mine Are think-ing of

Andante.

mf

wan-der turns fond - ly to thee; For bright rests the sun on thy clear wind-ing
proud-ly and rich on thy hills; Thy maid-ens are fair, and thy yeo - men are
me and the days of "Auld lang syne;" And blest be the hour when, my pil - grim-age

wan-der turns fond - ly to thee; For bright rests the sun on thy clear wind-ing
proud-ly and rich on thy hills; Thy maid-ens are fair, and thy yeo - men are
me and the days of "Auld lang syne;" And blest be the hour when, my pil - grim-age

wan-der turns fond - ly to thee; For bright rests the sun on thy clear wind-ing
proud-ly and rich on thy hills; Thy maid-ens are fair, and thy yeo - men are
me and the days of "Auld lang syne;" And blest be the hour when, my pil - grim-age

streams, And soft o'er thy mead-ows the moon pours her beams. New Eng-land, New
strong, And thy riv - ers run blithe-ly thy val - leys a - mong. New Eng-land, New
o'er, I shall sit by that hearthstone and leave it no more. New Eng-land, New

streams, And soft o'er thy mead-ows the moon pours her beams.
strong, And thy riv - ers run blithe-ly thy val - leys a - mong.
o'er, I shall sit by that hearthstone and leave it no more.

streams, And soft o'er thy mead-ows the moon pours her beams.
strong, And thy riv - ers run blithe-ly thy val - leys a - mong.
o'er, I shall sit by that hearthstone and leave it no more.

Eng-land, The wan-der-er's heart turns in fond-ness to thee.
Eng-land, The wan-der-er's heart turns in fond-ness to thee.
Eng-land, My heart as I wan - der turns fond-ly to thee.

My home o'er the sea, The wan-der-er's heart turns in fond-ness to thee.
My home o'er the sea, The wan-der-er's heart turns in fond-ness to thee.
My home o'er the sea, My heart as I wan - der turns fond-ly to thee.

My home o'er the sea, The wan-der-er's heart turns in fond-ness to thee.
My home o'er the sea, The wan-der-er's heart turns in fond-ness to thee.
My home o'er the sea, My heart as I wan - der turns fond-ly to thee.

OUR NOBLE LAND.

Dr. Orpheus Everts.

Frank L. Bristow.
Arr. by F. E. Chapman.

Andante e sostenuto.

Thank God! For this our na - tive land! O'er which the wings of

peace are spread! Where plen - ty o - pens wide her hand,

rit. Fine.

And gives to all sus - tain - ing bread! Our land, the land of

Free - dom still, Where hands and hearts and minds are free! Where no

en - e - my en - slaves the will, And jus - tice rules from sea to sea!

Thank God! for this our na - tive land! O'er which the wings of

peace are spread! Where plen - ty o - pens wide her hand,

And gives to all sus - tain - ing bread! Once more, and yet a -

gain once more We raise our voi - ces, while our hearts beat high,

D.C. al Fine.

With love, thanksgiv - ing, joy and praise, To Him who rules o'er land and sea!

SPEED OUR REPUBLIC!

THE AMERICAN HYMN.

Words and Music by Matthias Keller (1813–1890).

1. Speed our Re-pub-lic, O Fa-ther on high!
2. Fore-most in bat-tle, for Free-dom to stand,
3. Faith-ful and hon-est to friend and, to foe,

Lead us in path-ways of jus-tice and right; Rul-ers as
We rush to arms when a-roused by its call; Still as of
Will-ing to die in hu-man-i-ty's cause; Thus we de-

well as the ruled, "One and all," Gir-dle with vir-tue the
yore, when George Wash-ing-ton led, Thun-ders our war-cry, "We
fy all ty-ran-ni-cal pow'r, While we con-tend for our

ar - mor of might! Hail! three times hail to our coun - try and flag!
con - quer or fall!" Hail! three times hail to our coun - try and flag!
Un - ion and laws! Hail! three times hail to our coun - try and flag!

CHORUS. *cres.*
1ST AND 2D SOPRANO.

Rul - ers as well as the ruled, "One and all", Gir - dle with vir - tue the
Still as of yore when George Washing-ton led, Thun - ders our war - cry, "We
Thus we de - fy all ty - ran - ni - cal pow'r, While we con - tend for our

ALTO-TENOR. *cres.*

Ru - lers as well as the ruled, "One and all" Gir - dle with vir - tue the
Still as of yore, when George Washing-ton led, Thun - ders our war - cry, "we
Thus we de - fy all ty - ran - ni - cal pow'r, While we con - tend for our

TENOR AND BASS.

ar - mor of might! Hail, three times hail to our coun - try and flag!
con - quer or fall!". Hail, three times hail to our coun - try and flag!
Un - ion and laws! Hail, three times hail to our coun - try and flag!

ar - mor of might. Hail, three times hail to our coun - try and flag!
con - quer or fall!" Hail, three times hail to our coun - try and flag!
Un - ion and laws! Hail, three times hail to our coun - try and flag!

TO THEE WE SING, O COLUMBIA!

A. Peron.
Arr. by F. E. Chapman.

Maestoso.

To thee we sing, O Co-lum-bia! Thou home of the brave and the

free! Our trib-ute bring, bless-ed coun-try! And of-fer it glad-ly to

The won-d'ring na - - tions thy great-'ness praise, ... The won-d'ring
thee! The won-d'ring na - tions thy great-ness praise, . . . The

na - - tions thy great-ness praise,
won-d'ring na - tions thy great-ness praise, . While loy-al hearts their hom-age

raise, While loy-al hearts their grate - ful hom-age raise. Fine.

1. Thou, O Colum - bia, bring-est pro - tec - tion To the sons, the sons of sor-row and
2. Now will thy chil - dren faith-ful - ly guard thee, All their tho'ts, their tho'ts thy good shall em -

care; So will they of - fer will-ing af-fec-tion, So all thy last-ing praise de -
ploy; Glad will they la - bor thus to re-ward thee, As count-less bless-ings they en -

clare. If the hour of tri - al shall reach thee, Bur - ied
joy. Pride of all in hon - or thou reign - est, Hold - ing

deeds shall rise to thy aid; By clus - ter - ing friends then heav'n will
thus su - prem-est con - trol; And ev - er thy sway thou still main -

teach thee, Truth and kind - ness shall nev - er fade. . .
tain - - est, Though a - round thee the clouds may roll. . .

TO THEE, O COUNTRY!
NATIONAL HYMN.

Anna Eichberg King.

Julius Eichberg.
Arr. for schools by Samuel W. Cole.

Andante. ♩ = 69.

p   *cres.*   *marcato.*   *dim.*   *p*

Ped.   * Ped.   * Ped.   *

1ST AND 2D SOPRANO.

ppp

1. To thee, O coun - try, great and free, With trust - ing hearts we
2. For thee we dai - ly work and strive, To thee we give our

ALTO-TENOR.

ppp

1. To thee, O coun - try, great and free, With trust - ing hearts we
2. For thee we dai - ly work and strive, To thee we give our

TENOR AND BASS

ppp

p

cling; .... Our voi - - ces tuned by joy - ous love, Thy
love; .... For thee .. with fer - vor deep we pray To

p

cling; .... Our voi - - ces tuned by joy - ous love, Thy
love; .... For thee .. with fer - vor deep we pray To

p

ff   *p*

Thy pow'r and prais - es sing, ... Thy pow'r . . . . . and prais - es
To Him who dwells a - bove, ... To Him . . . . . who dwells a -
f
dim.
ppp
pow'r . . and prais - es sing, ... Thy pow'r and prais - es
Him . . who dwells a - bove, ... Who dwells . . . . a -
pow'r . . and prais - es sing, ... Thy pow'r and prais - es
Him . . who dwells a - bove, ... Who dwells . . . . a -
sing. Up - on . . thy might - y faith - ful heart, We
bove. O God, . pre-serve our fa - ther-land, Let
ff
sing. Up - on . . thy might - y faith - ful
bove. O God, . preserve our fa - ther -
marcato.

lay, . . we lay our bur - dens down,   Thou   art . . the on - ly
Peace, . let Peace its rul - er be,   And   let . . her hap - py

heart,   We   lay . . our burdens down, Thou art . . the on - ly
land,   Let   Peace . its rul - er be, And let . . her hap - py

friend . . who feels their   weight with - out . . a frown.   Up -
king - - - dom stretch from   north . to south - most sea.   O

friend . . who feels their   weight with - out . . a frown.
king - - - dom stretch from   north . to south - most sea.

.on . . thy might - y faith - ful heart,   We   lay, . . we lay our bur - dens
God, . pre - serve our fa - ther - land,   Let   Peace, . let Peace its rul - er

Up - on . . thy might - y faith - ful heart,   We
O   God, . pre - serve our fa - ther - land,   Let

down, Thou art . . the on - ly friend . . who feels their
be, And let . . her hap - py king - dom stretch from

lay . . our burdens down, Thou art . . the on - ly friend . . who feels their
Peace . her rul - er be, And let . . her hap - py king - dom stretch from

weight . with-out a . . frown. For
north . . to south - most

sea, From

weight . with-out a . . frown. For
north . . to south - most sea, From

north to south - most sea. . . . .

north to south - most sea. . . . .

OUR NATIVE LAND.

M. H. Cross.

A. Billeter. Arr. by W. A. F.

1. With hearts now touched by ten - d'rest feel - ings, Oh, let us praise our na - tive
2. Let ev - 'ry bless - ing now shed its fra - grance, And peace and plen - ty o'er us

land; For her we'll sing our no - blest songs, And lav - ish gifts with o - pen
shower; Let health and hap - pi - ness at - tend us, Till all have felt their mag - ic

hand. . Oh, land with all .... thy no - ble for - ests, Thy plains where
power. . Oh, may the bond . . . of faith and kind - ness For ev - er

hand. . Oh, land with all .... thy no - ble for - ests, Thy
power. . Oh, may the bond . . . of faith and kind - ness, For

hand. . Oh, land with all .... thy no - ble for - ests, Thy
power. . Oh, may the bond . . . of faith and kind - ness, For

rug - - - ged moun - tains stand. . . . With God's pure sky . .
hold . . . us in its hand. . . . While all thy sons . .

plains where rug - ged moun - tains stand. . . . With God's pure sky . .
ev - er hold us in its hand. . . . While all thy sons . .

plains where rug - ged moun - tains stand. . . . With God's pure sky . .
ev - er hold us in its hand. . . . While all thy sons . .

blue man-tling o'er   us, Heav'n bless thee, our na - tive land!   With God's pure
shall sing re - joic - ing, Heav'n bless thee, our na - tive land!   While all thy

blue man-tling o'er   us, Heav'n bless thee, our na - tive land!   With God's pure
shall sing re - joic - ing, Heav'n bless thee, our na - tive land!   While all thy

blue man-tling o'er   us, Heav'n bless thee, our na - tive land!   With God's pure
shall sing re - joic - ing, Heav'n bless thee, our na - tive land!   While all thy

sky . blue man - tling o'er   us, Heav'n bless thee,   our   na - - - tive land! .
sons shall sing   re - joic - ing, Heav'n bless thee,   our   na - - - tive land! .

sky . blue man - tling o'er   us, Heav'n bless thee,   our   na - - - tive land! .
sons shall sing   re - joic - ing, Heav'n bless thee,   our   na - - - tive land! .

sky . blue man - tling o'er   us, Heav'n bless thee,   our   na - - - tive land! .
sons shall sing   re - joic - ing, Heav'n bless thee,   our   na - - - tive land! .

OUR FLAG

OUR VICTORIOUS BANNER.

(*Composed for the World's Peace Jubilee.*)

DEXTER SMITH.

Sir JULIUS BENEDICT (1804–1885).
Arr. for schools by W. A. F.

Maestoso mia marziale.

1ST AND 2D SOPRANO.

O'er the high and o'er the low - ly, Floats that ban - ner bright and

ALTO-TENOR.

O'er the high and o'er the low - ly, Floats that ban - ner bright and

TENOR AND BASS.

O'er the high and o'er the low - ly, Floats that ban - ner bright and

ho - ly, In the rays of Free - dom's sun, In the rays of Free - dom's

ho - ly, In the rays of Free - dom's sun, In the rays of Free - dom's

ho - ly, In the rays of Free - dom's sun, In the rays of Free - dom's sun. In the na-tion's heart im-bed - ded, O'er our Un - ion new - ly

sun. In the na-tion's heart im-bed - ded, O'er our Un - ion new - ly

sun. In the na-tion's heart im-bed - ded, O'er our Un - ion new - ly

wed - ded, One in all, and all in one, One in all, and all in

wed - ded, One in all, and all in one, One in all, and all in

wed - ded, One in all, and all in one, One in all, and all in

one, O'er a Un - ion new - ly wed - ded, One in all, and all in one.

one, O'er a Un - ion new - ly wed - ded, One in all, and all in one.

one, O'er a Un - ion new - ly wed - ded, One in all, and all in one.

SOLO, OR SOPRANOS IN UNISON.
p
Let that
ban - ner wave for ev - er, May its lus - trous stars fade
p
nev - er, Till the stars shall pale on high, ... Till the
stars shall pale on high.
CHORUS.
Let that ban - ner wave for
Let that ban - ner wave for
Let that ban - ner wave for
8va

ev - - er, May its lus - trous stars fade nev - - er, Till the
ev - - er, May its lus - trous stars fade nev - - er, Till the
ev - - er, May its lus - trous stars fade nev - - er, Till the
8va.
cres.
dim.
stars shall pale on high, Till the stars shall pale on
stars shall pale on high, Till the stars shall pale on
stars shall pale on high, Till the stars shall pale on
8va.
Solo, or Sopranos in Unison.
high. While there's right the wrong de - feat - - ing, While there's
high.
high.

hope in true hearts beat - - - ing, Truth and free-dom shall not

die, Truth and free - dom shall not die, Truth and free - dom shall not

die, Truth and free - dom shall not die. . . . .

Chorus.

As it float - ed long be - fore us, Be it ev - er float - ing

As it float - ed long be - fore us, Be it ev - er float - ing

As it float - ed long be - fore us, Be it ev - er float - ing o'er us, O'er our land from shore to shore, O'er our land from shore to

o'er us, O'er our land from shore to shore, O'er our land from shore to

o'er us, O'er our land from shore to shore, O'er our land from shore to

shore. There are free-men yet to wave it, Mil-lions who will die to

shore. There are free-men yet to wave it, Mil-lions who will die to

shore. There are free-men yet to wave it, Mil-lions who will die to

save it, Wave it, save it ev-er-more, Wave it, save it ev-er-

save it, Wave it, save it ev-er-more, Wave it, save it ev-er-

save it, Wave it, save it ev-er-more, Wave it, save it ev-er-more, There are free - men yet to save . . it, save it,

more, There are free - men yet to save . . it, save it,

more, There are free - men yet to save . . it, save it,

save it ev - er - more, Wave it, save . . . . it

save it ev - er - more, Wave it, save . . . . it

save it ev - er - more, Wave it, save . . . . it

ev - er - more. . . . .

ev - er - more. . . . .

ev - er - more. . . . .

E PLURIBUS UNUM.

Words and Music by Capt. G. W. Cutter.   Arranged by Mrs. E. H. Pendleton.

Moderato.

1. Though man - y and bright are the stars that ap - pear In that
2. From the hour when those pa - tri - ots fear - less - ly flung That
3. The op - press'd of the earth to that stan - dard shall fly, Wher -
4. Tho' the old Al - le - ghe - ny may tow - er to heaven, And the
5. Then, up with our flag, let it stream on the air, Tho' our

flag by our coun - try un - furl'd, And the stripes that are swell - ing in
ban - ner of star - light a - broad, Ev - er true to them - selves, to that
ev - er its folds shall be spread; And the ex - ile shall feel 't is his
fa - ther of wa - ters di - vide; The links of our des - ti - ny
fa - thers are cold in their graves; They had hands that could strike, they had

ma - jes - ty there, Like a rain - bow a - dorn - ing the world. . . . .
mot - to they clung, As they clung to the prom - ise of God. . . . .
own na - tive sky, Where its stars shall float o - ver his ead. . . . .
can - not be riven While the truth of these words shall a - bide. . . . . .
souls that could dare, And their sons were not born to be slaves. . . . .

CHORUS.

1ST AND 2D SOPRANO.

Their   lights are un - sul - lied as those in the sky,   By a deed that our fa - thers have done;
By the bay - o - net traced at the mid - night of war, On the fields where our glo - ry was won;
And those stars shall in - crease, till the ful - ness of time   Its   mil - lions of cy - cles has run,
Then   oh! let them glow on each hel - met and brand, Tho' our blood like our riv - ers shall run;
Up,   up with that ban-ner, wher-e'er it may call   Our   mil-lions shall ral - ly a - round;

ALTO–TENOR.

Their   lights are un - sul - lied as those in the sky,   By a deed that our fa - thers have done;
By the bay - o - net traced at the mid - night of war, On the fields where our glo - ry was won;
And those stars shall in - crease, till the ful - ness of time   Its   mil - lions of cy - cles has run,
Then   oh! let them glow on each hel - met and brand Tho' our blood like our riv - ers shall run;
Up,   up with that ban-ner, wher-e'er it may call   Our   mil-lions shall ral - ly a - round;

TENOR AND BASS,

And they're leagued in as true and as ho - ly a tie, In their mot-to of "Man-y in one."
Oh!   per - ish the heart or the hand that would mar Our   mot-to   of "Man-y in one."
Till the world shall have welcomed its mission sub-lime, And the na-tions of earth shall be one.
Di - vide as we may in our own na - tive land, To the rest of the world we are one.
A   na - tion of free-men that moment shall fall, When its star shall be trailed on the ground.

And they're leagued in as true and as ho - ly a tie, In their mot-to of "Man-y in one."
Oh!   per - ish the heart or the hand that would mar Our   mot-to   of "Man-y in one."
Till the world shall have welcomed its mission sub-lime, And the na-tions of earth shall be one.
Di - vide as we may in our own na - tive land, To the rest of the world we are one.
A   na - tion of free-men that moment shall fall, When its star shall be trailed on the ground.

THE FLAG OF THE CONSTELLATION.

Thos. Buchanan Read (1822–1872).

Wm. Arms Fisher.

With spirit.

1. The stars of our morn on our ban - ner borne With the
2. What hand so bold to strike from its fold One
3. Its me - te - or form shall ride the storm, Till the
4. Peace, peace to the world, is our mot - to unfurled, Tho' we

i - ris of heav'n are blend - ded; The hands of our sires first
star or stripe of its bright - 'ning; To him be each star a
fierc - est of foes sur - ren - der; The storm gone by, it shall
shun not a field that is go - ry; At home or a - broad, fear - ing

min - gled those fires, By us they shall be de - fend - ed!
fier - y Mars, Each stripe a ter - rible light - ning.
gild the sky, As a rain - bow of peace and of splen - dor.
none but our God, We will carve our own path - way to glo - ry!

Copyright, MDCCCXCIX, by Oliver Ditson Company.

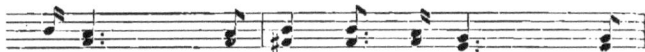

true, the Red, White, and Blue, The

true, ... the Red, White, and Blue, ... The

true, then hail the Red, White, and Blue, then hail the

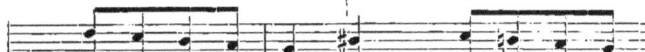

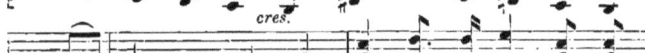

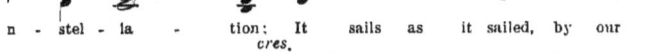

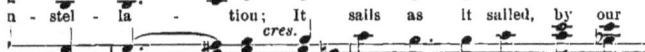

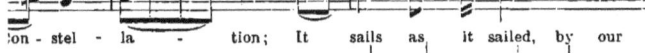

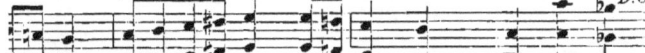

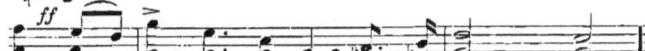

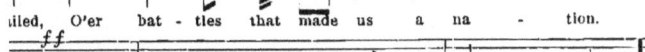

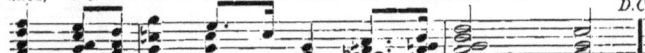

cres.

n - stel - la - tion; It sails as it sailed, by our

cres.

n - stel - la - tion; It sails as it sailed, by our

cres.

Con - stel - la - tion; It sails as it sailed, by our

cres.

D.C.

ff

ailed, O'er bat - tles that made us a na - tion.

ff

ailed, O'er bat - tles that made us a na - tion.

ff

ailed, O'er bat - tles that made us, that made us a na - tion.

D.C.

ff

FLAG OF THE FREE.

Richard Wagner (1813–1883).

1st and 2d Soprano.

Alto-Tenor.

1. Flag of the free, fair - est to see! Borne thro' the strife and the thun - der of war;
2. Flag of the brave, long may it wave, Cho - sen of God while His might we a - dore,

Tenor and Bass.

1. Flag of the free, fair - est to see! Borne thro' the strife and the thun - der of war;
2. Flag of the brave, long may it wave, Cho - sen of God while His might we a - dore,

1. Flag of the free, fair - est to see! Borne thro' the strife and the thun - der of war;
2. Flag of the brave, long may it wave, Cho - sen of God while His might we a - dore,

Ban - ner so bright, with star - ry light, Float ev - er proud - ly from moun - tain to shore;
In free-dom's van, for good to man, Sym - bol of right, thro' the years pass - ing o'er;

Ban - ner so bright, with star - ry light, Float ev - er proud - ly from moun - tain to shore;
In free-dom's van, for good to man, Sym - bol of right, thro' the years pass - ing o'er;

Ban - ner so bright, with star - ry light, Float ev - er proud - ly from moun - tain to shore;
In free-dom's van, for good to man, Sym - bol of right, thro' the years pass - ing o'er;

Em - blem of free - dom, hope to the slave, Spread thy fair folds to shield and to save,
Pride of our coun - try, hon - ored a - far, Scat - ter each cloud that dims but a star,

Em - blem of free - dom, hope to the slave, Spread thy fair folds to shield and to save,
Pride of our coun - try, hon - ored a - far, Scat - ter each cloud that dims but a star,

Em - blem of free - dom, hope to the slave, Spread thy fair folds to shield and to save,
Pride of our coun - try, hon - ored a - far, Scat - ter each cloud that dims but a star,

While thro' the sky, loud rings the cry, Un - ion and Lib - er - ty! One ev - er-more.

While thro' the sky, loud rings the cry, Un - ion and Lib - er - ty! One ev - er-more.

While thro' the sky, loud rings the cry, Un - ion and Lib - er - ty! One ev - er-more.

THE FLAG OF OUR UNION.

Geo. P. Morris

Wm. Vincent Wallace (1814-1865).

Maestoso con anima ma non troppo presto.
Moderato

1. "A song for our ban - ner," the
2. What God in His wis - dom and

watch - word re - call, Which gave the Re - pub - lic her sta - tion: "U -
mer - cy de - sign'd, And arm'd with His weap - ons of thun - der, Not

ni - ted we stand, di - vi - ded we fall!" It made and preserves us a na - tion!
all the earth's despots and fac - tions combin'd, Have the pow - er to con - quer or sun - der!

1ST AND 2D SOPRANO.

The un - ion of lakes, the un - ion of lands, The un - ion of states none can

ALTO-TENOR.

The un - ion of lakes, the un - ion of lands, The un - ion of states none can

TENOR & BASS.

The un - ion of lakes, the un - ion of lands, The un - ion of states none can

sev - er; The un - ion of hearts, The un - ion of hands, And the

sev - er; The un - ion of hearts, The un - ion of hands, And the

sev - er; The un - ion, The un - ion of hearts, The un - ion of hands, And the

ff

Flag of our Un - ion for ev - er, and ev - er! The Flag of our Un - ion for ev - er!

ff

Flag of our Un - ion for ev - er, and ev - er! The Flag of our Un - ion for ev - er!

ff

Flag of our Un - ion for ev - er, and ev - er! The Flag of our Un - ion for ev - er!

ff

Words and Music by CHARLES FONTEYN MANNEY.

In march tempo, with strongly marked rhythm.

1. Old Glo - ry a - gain now is wav - ing O'er free-men bound for the fight; For the just cause of Free-dom we're arm - ing, For the right we shall strike in our might. We are broth - ers who were foe - men, And we love our broad free land; She has

2. From the hill - side we come, from the val - ley, With our stargemm'd banner un-furled; To the sound of the bu - gle we ral - ly, And our tramp shall re - sound thro' the world. On-ward march, our coun - try needs us To a - venge the wrong at our gates; On - ward

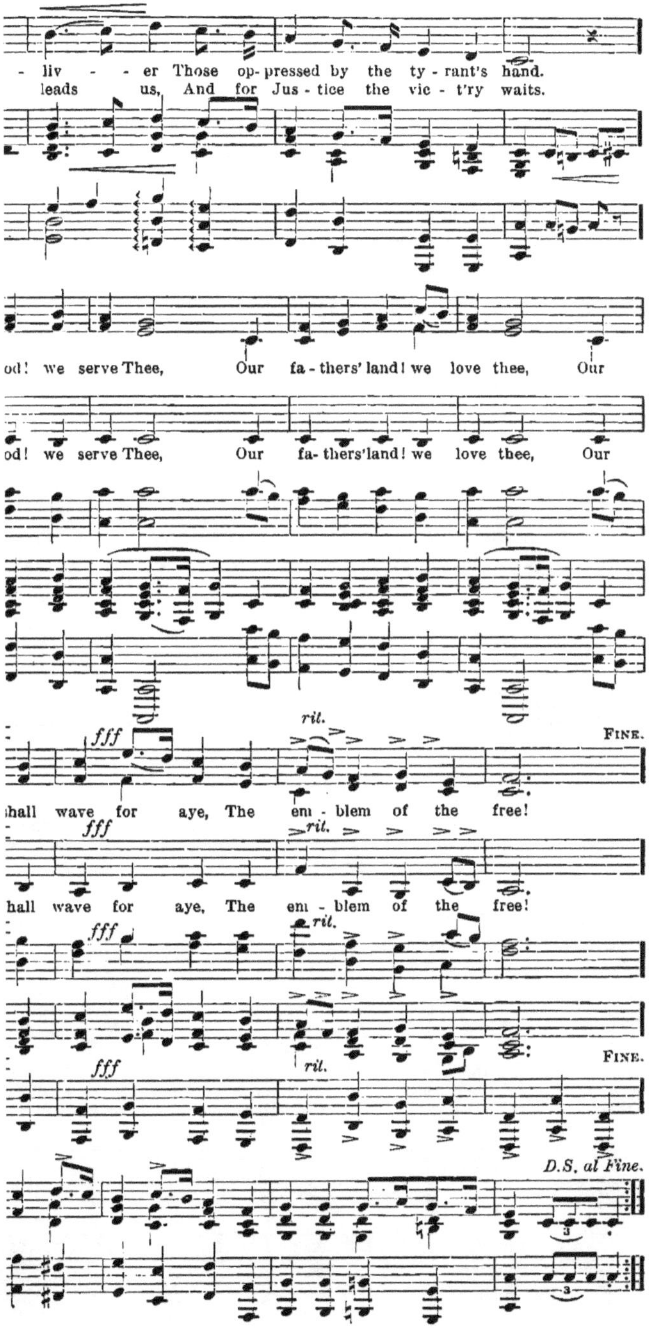

OUR FLAG AND MOTHER-LAND.

C. E. S. Wood.

Wm. Arms Fisher.

In march time, with spirit.

1. Fling out   our ban - ner to   the
2. No North!   no South!   no East!   no
3. For home   and right we live   and

air,   Go place   it   in   the wait - ing sky;   'Tis   Lib - er - ty's own
West!   Our coun - try nev - er shall di - vide;   We   are   the breth - ren
die,   For home   and right our fa - thers bled;   God   keep   our land in

bla - zon there, And   dear   to ev - 'ry pa - triot eye.   Be
of   thy breast, Great Moth - er - land! Our hope, our pride!   Call
pu - ri - ty When   we   too sleep a - mong the dead!   Hold

lov - ed flag   our fa - thers wove   In pain   from he - roes' blood - y shrouds,   Float
out   thy hosts, count all   thy sons;   Not an - y   one   of us shall fall,   By
us heart-clean while rage the wars!   And make   the ty - rant fear our blow!   God,

ff

glo - ri - ous! Thy chil - dren's love Ex - alts thee o'er the roll - ing clouds.
land or sea, when belch the guns, And Death is bu - sy with his flail.
save our flag, the Stripes and Stars, While yet the sea doth ebb and flow.

CHORUS.

1ST AND 2D SOPRANO.

By land and sea, we'll fight, and pray, and die, With the dear old flag a - bove us; And

ALTO.

By land and sea, we'll fight, and pray, and die, With the dear old flag a - bove us; And

TENOR.

By land and sea, we'll fight, and pray, and die, With the dear old flag a - bove us; And

BASS.

woe to the foe who hears our battle cry, "The flag! the flag! and those who love us."

woe to the foe who hears our battle cry, "The flag! the flag! and those who love us."

woe to the foe who hears our battle cry, "The flag! the flag! and those who love us."

OUR FLAG IS THERE.

This song was written by an Officer of the American Navy during the war of 1812. It being very popular, although long out of print, it was reprinted at the request of many Officers in the U. S. Navy.

New edition, edited by F. W.

1. Our Flag is there! Our Flag is there! We'll hail it with three loud huz-zas! Our
2. That flag withstood the bat - tle's roar, With foe - men stout, with foe - men brave; Strong

Flag is there! Our Flag is there! Be - hold the glo - rious Stripes and Stars! Stout
hands have sought that flag to low'r, And found a speed - y wat - 'ry grave. That

hearts have fought for that bright flag, Strong hands sus-tained it mast - head high, And
flag is known on ev - 'ry shore, The stand - ard of a gal - lant band; A -

oh! to see how proud it waves, Brings tears of joy in ev - 'ry eye.
like un-stained in peace or war, It floats o'er free - dom's hap - py land.

CHORUS.
1ST AND 2D SOPRANO.

Our Flag is there! Our Flag is there! We'll hail it with three

ALTO–TENOR.

Our Flag is there! Our Flag is there! We'll hail it with three

TENOR AND BASS.

loud huz - zas! Our Flag is there! Our Flag is there! Be -

loud huz - zas! Our Flag is there! Our Flag is there! Be -

hold the glo - rious Stripes and Stars!

hold the glo - rious Stripes and Stars!

RALLY ROUND THE FLAG.

James T. Fields (1817-1881).   William B. Bradbury.

Allegro con spirito.

Ral - ly round the flag, boys, Give it to the breeze, That's the ban - ner we love,

On the land and seas; Brave hearts are un - der our's, Hearts that heed no brag,

Gal - lant lads, fire a - way! And fight for the flag! Gal - lant lads, fire a - way! And

f — ff   *f — ff*

fight for the flag! Ral - ly round the flag, boys, Give it to the breeze,

3   3   3   3

That's the ban - ner we love, On the land and seas. Let our col - ors fly, boys,

Guard them day and night, For vic - to - ry is lib - er - ty, And

God will bless the right! Then ral - ly round the flag, boys,

Ral - ly round, ral - ly round, Ral - ly round the flag, boys, Ral - ly round the flag!

CHORUS.
1ST AND 2D SOPRANO.

Repeat pp

Ral - ly round the flag, boys, Ral - ly round, ral - ly round, Ral - ly round the flag, boys, Ral - ly round the flag!

ALTO-TENOR.

Ral - ly round the flag, boys, Ral - ly round, ral - ly round, Ral - ly round the flag, boys, Ral - ly round the flag!

TENOR AND BASS.

Ral - ly round the flag, boys, Ral - ly round, ral - ly round, Ral - ly round the flag, boys, Ral - ly round the flag!

Repeat pp

THE STAR SPANGLED BANNER.

Francis Scott Key (1779–1843). Samuel Arnold (1740–1802).

Con spirito.

mf

1. Oh! say, can you see by the dawn's ear - ly light, What so proud - ly we
2. On the shore, dim - ly seen thro' the mist of the deep, Where the foe's haught - y
3. And where is that band who so vaunt - ing - ly swore, 'Mid the hav - oc of
4. Oh! thus be it ev - er when free men shall stand Be - tween their loved

hail'd at the twi - light's last gleaming, Whose stripes and bright stars, thro' the per - il - ous
host in dread si - lence re - pos - es, What is that which the breeze, o'er the tow - er - ing
war and the bat - tle's con - fu - sion, A home and a coun - try they'd leave us no
home and the war's des - o - la - tion; Blest with vic - t'ry and peace, may the heav'n-res - cued

fight, O'er the ram-parts we watch'd, were so gal - lant - ly stream - ing? And the rock - et's red
steep, As it fit - ful - ly blows, half con - ceals, half dis - clos - es? Now it catch - es the
more? Their blood has wash'd out their foul foot-step's pol - lu - tion. No ref - uge could
land Praise the Power that hath made and pre - served us a na - tion. Then con - quer we

glare, the bombs burst-ing in air, Gave proof thro' the night that our flag was still there!
gleam of the morn - ing's first beam, In full glo - ry re - flect - ed, now shines in the stream.
save the hire - ling and slave From the ter - ror of flight or the gloom of the grave.
must, when our cause it is just, And this be our mot - to: "In God is our trust."

1ST AND 2D SOPRANO.

Oh!　say,　does that　star span-gled ban-ner　　yet　　wave,　O'er the land　of the
'Tis the star　span-gled ban-ner,　Oh! long may　it　　wave,　O'er the land　of the
And the star　span-gled ban-ner　in tri-umph　doth　wave,　O'er the land　of the
And the star span-gled　ban-ner　in　tri-umph　shall　wave,　While the land　of the

ALTO-TENOR.

Oh!　say,　does that　star span-gled ban-ner　　yet　　wave,　O'er the land　of the
'Tis the star span-gled　ban-ner,　Oh! long may　it　　wave,　O'er the land　of the
And the star span-gled　ban-ner　in tri-umph　doth　wave,　O'er the land　of the
And the star span-gled　ban-ner　in　tri-umph　shall　wave,　While the land　of the

TENOR AND BASS.

Oh!　say,　does that　star spang-gled ban-ner　　yet　　wave,　O'er the land　of the
'Tis the star spang-ed　ban-ner,　Oh! long　may　it　wave,　O'er the land　of the
And the star spang-led　ban-ner　in　tri-umph　doth　wave,　O'er the land　of the
And the star spang-led　ban-ner　in　tri-umph　shall　wave,　While the land　of the

free and the　home of the　brave!
free and the　home of the　brave!
free and the　home of the　brave!
free is　the　home of the　brave!

free and the home　of the　brave!
free and the home　of the　brave!
free and the home　of the　brave!
free is　the　home of the　brave!

free and the　home of the　brave!
free and the　home of the　brave!
free and the　home of the　brave!
free is　the　home of the　brave!

UNFURL THE GLORIOUS BANNER.

(The first part may be sung as a solo, if preferred.)

WM. B. BRADBURY.

Arr. for schools by SAMUEL W. COLE.

March movement.

1. Un - furl the glo - rious ban - ner, and fling it to the breeze, The
2. The glo - rious band of pa - triots who gave the flag its birth, Have
3. Ah! proud - ly should we bear it, and guard this flag of ours, Borne
4. The me - teor flag of seven - ty - six, long may it wave in pride, To

em - blem of our coun - try's pride, on land and on the seas, The
writ with steel in his - to - ry the re - cord of its worth; From
brave - ly in its in - fan - cy, a - midst the dark - er hours; For
tell the world how no - bly the pa - triot fa - thers died; When

em - blem of our lib - er - ty, borne proud - ly in the wars, The
east to west, from sea to sea, from pole to trop - ic sun, Will
on - ly the brave may bear it, a guar - dian it shall be For
from the shad - ows of their night out - burst the bril - liant sun, As

em - blem of our lib - er - ty, borne proud - ly in the wars, The
east to west, from sea to sea, from pole to trop - ic sun, Will
on - ly the brave may bear it, a guar - dian it shall be For
from the shad - ows of their night out - burst the bril - liant sun, As

em - blem of our lib - er - ty, borne proud - ly in the wars, The
east to west, from sea to sea, from pole to trop - ic sun, Will
on - ly the brave may bear it, a guar - dian it shall be For
from the shad - ows of their night out - burst the bril - liant sun, As

hope of ev - 'ry free - man, the gleam - ing stripes and stars!
eyes grow bright and hearts throb high, at the name of Wash - ing - ton.
those who well have won the right to boast of lib - er - ty.
bathed in light the stripes and stars, and lo! the field was won!

hope of ev - 'ry free - man, the gleam - ing stripes and stars!
eyes grow bright and hearts throb high, at the name of Wash - ing - ton.
those who well have won the right to boast of lib - er - ty.
bathed in light the stripes and stars, and lo! the field was won!

hope of ev - 'ry free - man, the gleam - ing stripes and stars!
eyes grow bright and hearts throb high, at the name of Wash - ing - ton.
those who well have won the right to boast of lib - er - ty.
bathed in light the stripes and stars, and lo! the field was won!

Un - furl the glo - rious ban - ner up - on the wel - com - ing air,

Un - furl the glo - rious ban - ner up - on the wel - com - ing air,

Un - furl the glo - rious ban - ner up - on the wel - com - ing air,

Read the rec - ord of the old - en time up - on its ra - diance there;

Read the rec - ord of the old - en time up - on its ra - diance there;

Read the rec - ord of the old - en time up - on its ra - diance there;

In bat - tle it has led us all on to vic - to - ry, Our

In bat - tle it has led us all on to vic - to - ry, Our

In bat - tle it has led us all on to vic - to - ry, Our

bea - con light to glo - ry, and shall it not still be,

bea - con light to glo - ry, and shall it not still be,

bea - con light to glo - ry, and shall it not still be,

Our ban - ner, our ban - ner, our glo - rious, glo - rious ban - ner, The

Our ban - ner, our ban - ner, our glo - rious, glo - rious ban - ner, The

Our ban - ner, our ban - ner, our glo - rious, glo - rious ban - ner, The

ban - ner of the free, the ban - ner of the free.

ban - ner of the free, the ban - ner of the free.

ban - ner of the free, the ban - ner of the free.

THERE'S A BEAUTIFUL FLAG.

TRIO AND CHORUS.

Words by BENJ. WEBBER.
GEO. F. WILSON.

1ST SOPRANO.

1. There's a beau - ti - ful flag in the land of the free, There's a
2. There's a beau - ti - ful flag on the sol - dier boy's grave; For its
3. There's a beau - ti - ful flag on the snow - cov - er'd height, And it
4. There's a beau - ti - ful flag that we all love to se. 'Tis the

2D SOPRANO.

1. There's a beau - ti - ful flag in the land of the free, There's a
2. There's a beau - ti - ful flag on the sol - dier boy's grave; For its
3. There's a beau - ti - ful flag on the snow - cov - er'd height, And it
4. There's a beau - ti - ful flag that we all love to see, 'Tis the

ALTO.

1. There's a beau - ti - ful flag in the land of the free, There's a
2. There's a beau - ti - ful flag on the sol - dier boy's grave; For its
3. There's a beau - ti - ful flag on the snow - cov - er'd height, And it
4. There's a beau - ti - ful flag that we all love to see, 'Tis the

beau - ti - ful flag on the treach - er - ous sea; Through the
light, silk - en text - ure his young life he gave; And it
wel - comes the dawn with its red, ro - sy light; It is
old flag of free - dom, the gift of the free; All un -

beau - ti - ful flag on the treach - er - ous sea; Through the
light, silk - en text - ure his young life he gave; And its
wel - comes the dawn, with its red, ro - sy light; It is
old flag of free - dom, the gift of the free; All un -

beau - ti - ful flag on the treach - er - ous sea; Through the
light, silk - en text - ure his young life he gave; And it
wel - comes the dawn, with its red, ro - sy light; It is
old flag of free - dom, the gift of the free; All un -

THERE'S A BEAUTIFUL FLAG.

black - ness of night, o'er the dark swol - len wave, Floats that
waves o'er his form, in the light, breez - y air, When the
tossed by the wind, where it waves o'er the main, On the
furl'd in the breeze, with its silk all un - roll'd, There are

black - ness of night, o'er the dark swol - len wave, Floats that
waves o'er his form, in the light, breez - y air, When the
tossed by the wind, where it waves o'er the main, On the
furl'd in the breeze, with its silk all un - roll'd, There are

black - ness of night, o'er the dark swol - len wave, Floats that
waves o'er his form, in the light, breez - y air, When the
tossed by the wind, where it waves o'er the main, On the
furl'd in the breeze, with its silk all un - roll'd, There are

shel - ter - ing flag, o'er the true and the brave.
sweet - scent - ed flow - ers of sum - mer are there.
bleak, breez - y peak of the rough, rock - y chain.
clus - ters of stars on this flag of the bold.

shel - ter - ing flag, o'er the true and the brave.
sweet - scent - ed flow - ers of sum - mer are there.
bleak, breez - y peak of the rough, rock - y chain.
clus - ters of stars on this flag of the bold.

shel - ter - ing flag, o'er the true and the brave.
sweet - scent - ed flow - ers of sum - mer are there.
bleak, breez - y peak of the rough, rock - y chain.
clus - ters of stars on this flag of the bold.

CHORUS.
1ST AND 2D SOPRANO.

Where the fierce tem - pest raves on the wild, storm - y sea, Floats the
And it droops o'er the grave of the he - ro be - low, When the
'Tis the flag of our coun - try,— the red, white, and blue,— To its
Yes, we love it, we love it, dear flag of the free, It is

ALTO–TENOR.

Where the fierce tem - pest raves on the wild, storm - y sea, Floats the
And it droops o'er the grave of the he - ro be - low, When the
'Tis the flag of our coun - try,— the red, white, and blue,— To its
Yes, we love it, we love it, dear flag of the free, It is

TENOR AND BASS.

Where the fierce tem - pest raves on the wild, storm - y sea, Floats the
And it droops o'er the grave of the he - ro be - low, When the
'Tis the flag of our coun - try,— the red, white, and blue,— To its
Yes, we love it, we love it, dear flag of the free, It is

stars and the stripes from the land of the free.
mound that was green lies en - shroud - ed in snow.
stars and its stripes we will ev - er be true.
dear to our hearts, and our pride it shall be.

stars and the stripes from the land of the free.
mound that was green lies en - shroud - ed in snow.
stars and its stripes we will ev - er be true.
dear to our hearts, and our pride it shall be.

stars and the stripes from the land of the free.
mound that was green lies en - shroud - ed in snow.
stars and its stripes we will ev - er be true.
dear to our hearts, and our pride it shall be.

OUR NAVY

THE BANNER OF THE SEA.

Words by Homer Greene.　　　　　　　　　Music by H. G. Ganss.

1. By wind and wave the sail - or brave has fared To shores of ev - 'ry
2. Co - lum-bia's men were they who then went down, Not knights nor kings of
3. With hearts of oak, thro' storm and smoke and flame, Co - lum - bia's sea - men
4. Our flag we cheer, that nev - er fear may ride On an - y wave with

sea; . . . . But, nev - er yet have sea - men met or dared Grim
old; . . . . But bright-er far their lau - rels are than crown Or
long; . . . . Have brave - ly fought and no - bly wrought that shame Might
thee, ... Thou ship of state whose tim - bers great a - bide The

death for vic - to - ry In brav - er mood than they who died On drift-ing decks, in
cor - o - net of gold. Our sail - or true, of an - y crew, Would give the last long
nev - er dull their song. They sing the coun-try of the free, The glo - ry of the
home of lib - er - ty; For, so, our gal - lant Yan - kee tars, Of dar - ing deeds and

o - cean's tide, While cheer - ing ev - 'ry sail - or's pride, The Ban - ner of the
breath he drew To cheer the old red, white, and blue, The Ban - ner of the
roll - ing sea, The star - ry flag of lib - er - ty, The Ban - ner of the
hon - ored scars, Will make the Ban - ner of the Stars The Ban - ner of the

Free! While cheer - ing ev - 'ry sail - or's pride, The Ban - ner of the Free!
Bold! To cheer the old red, white, and blue, The Ban - ner of the Bold!
Strong! The star - ry flag of lib - er - ty, The Ban - ner of the Strong!
Sea! Will make the Ban - ner of the Stars The Ban - ner of the Sea!

CHORUS. *Risoluto.*

1ST AND 2D SOPRANO.

The Ban - ner of the Free! . . . The Ban - ner of the Free! . . . While
The Ban - ner of the Bold! . . . The Ban - ner of the Bold! . . . To
The Ban - ner of the Strong! . . The Ban - ner of the Strong! . . The
The Ban - ner of the Sea! . . . The Ban - ner of the Sea! . . . Will

ALTO–TENOR.

The Ban - ner of the Free! . . . The Ban - ner of the Free! . . . While
The Ban - ner of the Bold! . . The Ban - ner of the Bold! . . . To
The Ban - ner of the Strong! . . The Ban - ner of the Strong! . . The
The Ban - ner of the Sea! . . . The Ban - ner of the Sea! . . . Will

TENOR AND BASS.

poco riten. ff

cheer-ing ev - 'ry   sail - or's pride, The Ban - ner   of   the   Free!   While
cheer the old   red, white, and blue, The Ban - ner   of   the   Bold!   To
star - ry flag of   lib - er - ty,   The Ban - ner   of   the   Strong! The
make the Ban - ner   of   the Stars The Ban - ner   of   the   Sea!   Will

poco riten. ff

cheer-ing ev - 'ry   sail - or's pride, The Ban - ner   of   the   Free!   While
cheer the old   red, white, and blue, The Ban - ner   of   the   Bold!   To
star - ry flag of   lib - er - ty,   The Ban - ner   of   the   Strong! The
make the Ban - ner   of   the Stars The Ban - ner   of   the   Sea!   Will

poco riten. ff

ff poco riten.

cheer-ing ev - 'ry   sail - or's pride, The Ban - ner   of   the   Free!
cheer the old   red, white, and blue, The Ban - ner   of   the   Bold!
star - ry flag of   lib - er - ty,   The Ban - ner   of   the   Strong!
make the Ban - ner   of   the Stars The Ban - ner   of   the   Sea!

cheer-ing ev - 'ry   sail - or's pride, The Ban - ner   of   the   Free!
cheer the old   red, white, and blue, The Ban - ner   of   the   Bold!
star - ry flag of   lib - er - ty,   The Ban - ner   of   the   Strong!
make the Ban - ner   of   the Stars The Ban - ner   of   the   Sea!

p a tempo.

f

THE FREEDOM OF THE SEAS.

Words written in 1813. Author unknown.

WM. ARMS FISHER.

1. Ye sons of free Co - lum - bi - a, whose fa - thers dared the
o'er her mist - y moun - tain tops, Co - lum - bia's ea - gle
lum - bus, first of mar - i - ners, to us be - queathed his
sires were Brit - ons, and 'tis Heav'n's im - mu - ta - ble de -
lum - bia's ea - gle flag shall fly all fear - less o'er the

waves, The bat - tle and the wil - der - ness, to shun the fate of slaves; The
soars, And sees two might - y o - ceans roll their trib - ute to her shores. Th' At -
name; The o - cean's first great con - quer - or re - signed to us his claim. From
cree, That sons of Brit - ons ne'er shall yield the free - dom of the sea. Our
flood, To ev - 'ry friend - ly name a dove, — to foes a bird of blood. We'll

rights they bled for we'll main - tain wher - e'er a wave can flow, And be
lan - tic and Pa - cif - ic wave for us a - like shall flow, We'll be
east to west, and round the globe, wher - e'er a wave can flow, We'll be
home as theirs is on the wave, and where a wave can flow, We'll be
bear the bless - ings of our law wher - e'er a wave can flow, And be

free on the sea in de - spite of ev - 'ry foe.

1ST AND 2D SOPRANO.

Tho' ty-rants frown and can-nons roar, and the an - gry tem - pests blow,   We'll be free on the

ALTO-TENOR.

Tho' ty-rants frown and can-nons roar, and the an - gry tem - pests blow,   We'll be free on the

TENOR AND BASS.

sea, We'll be free; We'll be free on the sea,   In de-spite   of ev - 'ry   foe we'll be

sea, We'll be free; We'll be free on the sea, on the sea, In de-spite of   ev - 'ry   foe we'll be

Verses 1, 2, 3, 4.   D.S. | *Verse 5.*

free   on   the   sea.

2. High sea.
3. Co -
4. Our
5. Co -

free   on   the   sea.

sea.

Verses 1, 2, 3, 4.   D.S. | *Verse 5.*

COLUMBIA'S BANNER ON THE SEA.

Author of words unknown.

WM. ARMS FISHER.

In march time.

1. Of all the flags that float a - loft O'er Nep - tune's gal - lant,
2. Be - neath its folds we fear no foe, Our hearts shall nev - er,
3. On ev - 'ry wave, on ev - 'ry shore, Co - lum - bia's flag shall
4. Its en - e - mies our own shall be, Up - on the land or

gal - lant tars, That wave on high in vic - to - ry, A - bove the sons of
nev - er quail; With bo - soms bare the storm we'll dare, And brave the bat - tle
ev - er go, And thro' all time its fame sub - lime, With bright - er lines shall
on the main, Its star - ry light shall gild the fight, And guide its i - ron

Mars; Give us the flag, Co - lum - bia's flag, The em - blem of the
gale; So let it hail with shot and shell, The great guns boom and
glow; For Free - dom's stand - ard is our flag, Its guar - dians Free - dom's
rain; Nor for - eign pow'r, nor trea - son's arts Shall shake our Pa - triot

Whose flash - ing stars blaz'd thro' the wars, For truth and lib - er - ty.
Still through the fray all shall o - bey, That flag for ev - er - more.
And woe be-tide the in-sult - er's pride When we un - loose our guns.
While with our life in peace or strife, We'll keep the flag a - bove.

lads, in o - cean's brine, And give it three times three; And

lads, in o - cean's brine, And give it three times three; And

lads, in o - cean's brine, And give it three times three, times three, And

with song and shout, The Ban - ner of the Sea.

with song and shout, The Ban - ner of the Sea.

with song and shout, The Ban - ner of the Sea.

: sung in unison, if preferred.

Now give it three times three; Now give it three times three; And

Now give it three times three; Now give it three times three; And

Now give it three times three; Now give it three times three; And

fling it out with song and shout, Ban - ner of . . . the Sea.

fling it out with song and shout, Ban - ner of . . . the Sea.

fling it out with song and shout, Ban - ner of . . . the Sea.

OUR HEROES

(MEMORIAL DAY)

OUR NAVAL HEROES.

Marion Froelich.

G. Froelich.

Solemnly.

1ST AND 2D SOPRANO.

1. Not where the grass - es ver - dant, On round - ed hil - locks bed, Are
2. The wind moaned in the rig - ging, And tossed the o - cean's swell; It
3. And as we gath - er year - ly In hon - or of our dead, We'll

ALTO-TENOR.

1. Not where the grass - es ver - dant, On round - ed hil - locks bed, Are
2. The wind moaned in the rig - ging, And tossed the o - cean's swell; It
3. And as we gath - er year - ly In hon - or of our dead, We'll

TENOR AND BASS.

1. Not where the grass - es ver - dant, On round - ed hil - locks bed, Are
2. The wind moaned in the rig - ging, And tossed the o - cean's swell; It
3. And as we gath - er year - ly In hon - or of our dead, We'll

Solemnly.

laid our Na - val he - roes, Sleep soft our Na - vy's dead; But
sang a sol - emn re - quiem, And tolled a fu - n'ral knell; No
not for - get the He - roes That sleep in O - cean's bed; The

laid our Na - val he - roes, Sleep soft our Na - vy's dead; But
sang a sol - emn re - quiem, And tolled a fu - n'ral knell; No
not for - get the He - roes That sleep in O - cean's bed; The

laid our Na - val he - roes, Sleep soft our Na - vy's dead; But
sang a sol - emn re - quiem, And tolled a fu - n'ral knell; No
not for - get the He - roes That sleep in O - cean's bed; The

Copyright, MDCCCXCIV, by Oliver Ditson Company.

where the waves are rock - ing A - bove the path - less deep, Full
ten - der hand to bu - ry, No time for fare - well tear, No
Ar - my and the Na - vy That saved our lib - er - ty, Be

where the waves are rock - ing A - bove the path - less deep, Full
ten - der hand to bu - ry, No time for fare - well tear, No
Ar - my and the Na - vy That saved our lib - er - ty, Be

where the waves are rock - ing A - bove the path - less deep, Full
ten - der hand to bu - ry, No time for fare - well tear, No
Ar - my and the Na - vy That saved our lib - er - ty, Be

ma - ny a sol - dier sail - or Rests in his last long sleep.
lau - rel wreaths for crown - ing But those we of - fer here.
sung in song and sto - ry, As one on land or sea.

ma - ny a sol - dier sail - or Rests in his last long sleep.
lau - rel wreaths for crown - ing But those we of - fer here.
sung in song and sto - ry, As one on land or sea.

ma - ny a sol - dier sail - or Rests in his last long sleep.
lau - rel wreaths for crown - ing But those we of - fer here.
sung in song and sto - ry, As one on land or sea.

O, rock them gen - tly, O - cean, Our Na - val he - roes brave, Who

O, rock them gen - tly, O - cean, Our Na - val he - roes brave, Who

O, rock them gen - tly, O - cean, Our Na - val he - roes brave, Who

'mid the storm of bat - tle Their lives for free - dom gave. . .

'mid the storm of bat - tle Their lives for free - dom gave. . .

'mid the storm of bat' - tle Their lives for free - dom gave. . .

E'ER FADELESS BE THEIR GLORY.

HYMN FOR DECORATION DAY.

Words and adaptation by M. J. C.

FELIX MENDELSSOHN.

Place them a - bove each grave; These braves re-stored our na - tion, Our homes they died to
Soil'd not by foe - man's hand, This blood-bought flag of he - roes, Who loved their glorious
Hom - age to ren - der still; Our words of love and du - ty We glad - ly now ful -

Place them a - bove each grave; These braves re-stored our na - tion, Our homes they died to
Soil'd not by foe - man's hand, This blood-bought flag of he - roes, Who loved their glorious
Hom - age to ren - der still; Our words of love and du - ty We glad - ly now ful -

Place them a - bove each grave; These braves re-stored our na - tion, Our homes they
Soil'd not by foe - man's hand, This blood-bought flag of he - roes, Who loved their
Hom - age to ren - der still; Our words of love and du - ty We now, we

homes they died to save.
loved their glo - - rious land.
glad - ly now ful - fil.

save; Their deeds re - stored our na - tion, Our homes . . . they died to save.
land; This blood-bought flag of he - roes, Who loved . . . their glo - rious land.
fil; Our words of love and du - ty, We glad - ly now ful - fil.

save; Their deeds re - stored our na - tion, Our homes they died to save.
land; This blood-bought flag of he - roes, Who loved their glo - - rious land.
fil; Our words of love and du - ty, We glad - ly now ful - fil.

died to save; Their deeds restored our na - tion, Our homes they died to save.
glo - rious land; This blood-bought flag of he - roes, Who loved their glo - - rious land.
now ful - fil; Our words of love and du - ty, We glad - ly now ful - fil.

MEMORIAL HYMN.

Geo. F. Wilson.

Slow march time.

1ST AND 2D SOPRANO.

1. We vis - it the graves of the sol - diers to - day, While
2. Tho' stran - gers with com - rades now qui - et - ly sleep, The
3. Now an - thems of praise and thanks - giv - ing we sing, And

ALTO-TENOR.

1. We vis - it the graves of the sol - diers to - day, While
2. Tho' stran - gers with com - rades now qui - et - ly sleep, The
3. Now an - thems of praise and thanks - giv - ing we sing, And

TENOR AND BASS.

1. We vis - it the graves of the sol - diers to - day, While
2. Tho' stran - gers with com - rades now qui - et - ly sleep, The
3. Now an - thems of praise and thanks - giv - ing we sing, And

na - ture is robed with the beau - ty of May, We'll
soil where they rest we will or - der - ly keep, For
gar - lands and wreaths in pro - fu - sion we bring, And

na - ture is robed with the beau - ty of May, We'll
soil where they rest we will or - der - ly keep, For
gar - lands and wreaths in pro - fu - sion we bring, And

na - ture is robed with the beau - ty of May, We'll
soil where they rest we will or - der - ly keep, For
gar - lands and wreaths in pro - fu - sion we bring, And

car - ry of flow - ers the bright - est there, Of ten - der af - fec - tion the
in our great war they each took a part, The cause they de - fend - ed is
bless'd be the mem - 'ry of all comrades brave, Whose forms now are sleep - ing be -

car - ry of flow - ers the bright - est there, Of ten - der af - fec - tion the
in our great war they each took a part, The cause they de - fend - ed is
bless'd be the mem - 'ry of all comrades brave Whose forms now are sleep - ing be -

car - ry of flow - ers the bright - est there, Of ten - der af - fec - tion the
in our great war they each took a part, The cause they de - fend - ed is
bless'd be the mem - 'ry of all comrades brave Whose forms now are sleep - ing be -

em - blems so fair, Of ten - der af - fec - tion the em - blems so fair.
dear to our hearts, The cause they de - fend - ed is dear to our hearts.
neath in the grave, Whose forms now are sleep - ing be - neath in the grave.

em - blems so fair, Of ten - der af - fec - tion the em - blems so fair.
dear to our hearts, The cause they de - fend - ed is dear to our hearts.
neath in the grave, Whose forms now are sleep - ing be - neath in the grave.

em - blems so fair, Of ten - der af - fec - tion the em - blems so fair.
dear to our hearts, The cause they de - fend - ed is dear to our hearts.
neath in the grave, Whose forms now are sleep - ing be - neath in the grave.

PRO PATRIA.

TRIO, SOLO, AND CHORUS.

Words by GEORGE L. HEATH.

GEO. F. WILSON.

Andantino.

A cir-cle of flags that flut-ter In the shift-ing sum-mer breeze, . . Where the
And thus for our fall-en he-roes, Who rest in their name-less graves, . . The

walls of the si-lent cit-y Now rise 'neath the dark pine trees, Now
"red, white, and blue" is float-ing A-bove where the tall grass waves, A-

rise 'neath the dark pine trees. 1. With-in that sa-cred cir-cle, The
bove where the tall grass waves. 2. We may not deck with flow-ers Those

SOPRANO SOLO.

Hum accompaniment.

tall grass gen-tly waves, But on-ly bur-ied mem-'ries Lie in the clus-tered
graves a-far un-known, We may not rear a-bove them, The gleam-ing mar-ble

ril.

tempo.

graves; In depths of shad-ow-ing for-est, Or on sun-beat-en plain, Be-
stone; But nev-er while thou liv-est, O faith-ful mem-o-ry, Can

tempo.

Copyright, MDCCCLXXXVII, by F. H. GILSON.

neath the riv - ers flow - ing, Are the un - known graves of our slain.
we for - get our com - rades Who died to keep us free.

CHORUS.

1ST AND 2D SOPRANO.

And ev - 'ry wav - 'ring shad - ow Fall - eth up - on some home, Where
Yes, there's one spot most sa - cred, And dear un - to my heart, 'Tis

ALTO-TENOR.

And ev - 'ry wav - 'ring shad - ow Fall - eth up - on some home, Where
Yes, there's one spot most sa - cred, And dear un - to my heart, 'Tis

TENOR AND BASS.

And ev - 'ry wav - 'ring shad - ow Fall - eth up - on some home, Where
Yes, there's one spot most sa - cred, And dear un - to my heart, 'Tis

hearts call in the si - lence, For those who'll nev - er come.
where those flags are wav - ing On that cir - cle set a - part.

hearts call in the si - lence, For those who'll nev - er come.
where those flags are wav - ing On that cir - cle set a - part.

hearts call in the si - lence, For those who'll nev - er come.
where those flags are wav - ing On that cir - cle set a - part.

THE FLAG THEY LOVED SO WELL.

DUET AND CHORUS FOR MIXED VOICES.

GEORGE RUSSELL JACKSON.   HERBERT LESLIE.

1. A - gain the grass is grow - ing green,   Where sleep the no - ble brave,   A -
2. To bat - tle forth in bands they went   From an - vil, plow, and loom,   Old
3. Now com - rades bring the gar - lands fair   That crown the smil - ing May,   Where

gain we come with fra - grant flow'rs,   To deck each he - ro's grave;   In
age, and man-hood's strength and prime,   And youth's fair morn-ing bloom;   They
free - ly waves a - bove their graves   The star - ry flag to - day;   They

war they were their coun-try's shield,   And bore 'midst shot and shell,   On
bore their coun-try's flag a - loft,   And fight - ing for it fell,   The
speak a - bout the by - gone days,   And of their com - rades tell,   Who

man - y a crimsoned bat - tle field,   The flag they loved so well.
stars and stripes, the hon - ored flag,   The flag they loved so well.
bat - tled to de - fend the flag,   The flag they loved so well.

Chorus.
1st and 2d Soprano.

In war they were their coun-try's shield, And bore 'midst shot and shell, On

Alto-Tenor.

In war . they were their coun-try's shield, And bore 'midst shot and shell, On

Tenor and Bass.

In war they were their coun-try's shield, And bore 'midst shot and shell, On

man - y a crim-soned bat - tle field, The flag they loved so well.

man - y a crim-soned bat - tle field, The flag they loved so well.

man - y a crim-soned bat'- tle field, The flag they loved so well.

SOLDIER, REST! THY WARFARE OE'R.

Sir WALTER SCOTT (1771–1832).

WM. ARMS FISHER.
(Arranged from the original quartet for men's voices.)

Not too slow.

1ST AND 2D SOPRANO.

1. Sol - dier, rest! thy war - fare o'er, Sleep the sleep that knows not break-ing;
2. No rude sound shall reach thine ear, Ar - mor's clang, nor war - steed champing,

ALTO-TENOR.

1. Sol - dier, rest! thy war - fare o'er, Sleep the sleep that knows not break-ing;
2. No rude sound shall reach thine ear, Ar - mor's clang, nor war - steed champing,

TENOR AND BASS.

1. Sol - dier, rest! thy war - fare o'er, Sleep the sleep that knows not break-ing:
2. No rude sound shall reach thine ear, Ar - mor's clang, nor war - steed champing,

cres.

Dream of bat - tle - fields no more, Days of dan - ger, nights of wak - ing.
Trump nor pi - broch sum - mon here, Mus - t'ring clan, or squad - ron tramp-ing;

cres.

Dream of bat - tle - fields no more, Days of dan - ger, nights of wak - ing.
Trump nor pi - broch sum - mon here, Mus - t'ring clan, or squad-ron tramp-ing;

cres.

Dream of bat - tle - fields no more, Days of dan - ger, nights of wak - ing.
Trump nor pi - broch sum - mon here, Mus - t'ring clan, or squad - ron tramp-ing,

cres.

In our isle's en - chant - ed hall, Hands un - seen thy couch are strew-ing,
Yet the lark's shrill fife may come At the day - break, from the fal - low,

In our isle's en - chant - ed hall, Hands un - seen thy couch are strew-ing,
Yet the lark's shrill fife may come At the day - break, from the fal - low,

In our isle's en - chant - ed hall, Hands un - seen thy couch are strew-ing,
Yet the lark's shrill fife may come At the day - break, from the fal - low,

Soft - ly strains of mu - sic fall. . . Sol - dier, rest! thy war - fare o'er,
And the bit - tern sound his drum. . . Ru - der sounds shall none be near,

Soft - ly strains of mu - sic fall. . . . Sol - dier, rest! thy war - fare o'er,
And the bit - tern sound his drum. . . Ru - der sounds shall none be near,

Soft - ly strains of mu - sic fall. . . . Sol - dier, rest! thy war - fare o'er,
And the bit - tern sound his drum. . . Ru - der sounds shall none be near,

cres.

Sleep   the sleep that   knows   not break-ing; Dream   of   fight - ing fields   no   more;
Guards   nor ward - ers chal - lenge here;   Here   no   war - steed's neigh can   come.

cres.

Sleep   the sleep that knows   not break - ing; Dream   of   fight - ing fields   no   more;
Guards   nor ward - ers chal - lenge here;   Here   no   war - steed's neigh can   come.

cres.

Sleep   the sleep that knows   not break - ing; Dream   of   fight - ing fields   no   more;
Guards   nor ward - ers chal _ lenge here;   Here   no   war - steed's neigh can   come;

cres.

dim.

Sleep   the sleep that   knows   not break - ing; Morn   of   toil,   nor night   of wak - ing.

dim.

Sleep   the sleep that   knows   not break - ing; Morn   of   toil,   nor night   of wak - ing.

dim.

Sleep   the sleep that   knows   not break - ing, Morn   of   toil,   nor night   of wak - ing.

dim.

p et rit.   *pp*

Sleep   the   sleep   that knows not break - ing,   Sol - dier, rest!   Sol - dier, rest!

p et rit.   *pp*

Sleep   the   sleep   that knows not break - ing,   Sol - dier, rest!   Sol - dier, rest!

p et rit.   *pp*

Sleep   the   sleep   that knows not break - ing,   Sol - dier, rest!   Sol - dier, rest!

p et rit.   *pp*

TRIO.

Words by HEZEKIAH BUTTERWORTH.

GEO. F. WILSON.

In slow march time.

1. Play the peace bu - gles low, While the white ros - es blow, And the
2. Set the flag on their graves, Where the ver - nal wind laves The
3. Set the flag on their graves, And the thrush float - ing low, Shall

ap - ple blooms fill The green val - leys with snow; Let our sweet songs a - rise On the
ros - es of peace From the far west - ern waves; 'Tis for you and for me Their sweet
take up our song And sing on as we go, O'er the em - blem we leave 'Mid the

spring's western wind; We can nev - er for - get them Who died for man-kind.
lives they re-signed; They are broth - ers of all men Who died for man-kind.
lil - ies en-shrined; Their lives are im - mor - tal Who died for man-kind.

Chorus.

Set the flag on their graves, In the lil - ies en - shrined, We can
Set the flag on their graves, In the lil - ies en - shrined, They are
Set the flag on their graves, In the lil - ies en - shrined, Their . .

nev - er for - get them, Who died for man - kind.
broth - ers of all men Who died for man - kind.
lives are im - mor - tal, Who died for man - kind.

WM. COLLINS.

1ST AND 2D SOPRANO.

WM. ARMS FISHER.

Arranged from the original quartet for men's voices.

How sleep the brave, who sink to rest, By all their

ALTO-TENOR.

How sleep the brave, who sink to rest, By all their

TENOR-BASS.

How sleep the brave, who sink to rest, By all their

coun - try's wish - es blessed! When Spring with dew - y fin - gers

coun - try's wish - es blessed! When Spring with dew - y fin - gers

coun - try's wish - es blessed! When Spring with dew - y fin - gers

cres.

urns to deck their hal - lowed mould, She then shall

cres.

urns to deck their hal - lowed mould, She then shall

cres.

urns to deck their hal - lowed mould, She then shall

cres.

et - er sod Than fan - cy's feet have ev - er trod.

et - er sod Than fan - cy's feet have ev - er trod.

et - er sod Than fan - cy's feet have ev - er trod.

y hands their knell is rung; By forms un -

y hands their knell is rung; By forms un -

y hands their knell is rung; By forms un -

seen their dirge is sung; Here Hon-or comes, a pil-grim gray, To

seen their dirge is sung; Here Hon-or comes, a pil-grim gray, To

seen their dirge is sung; Here Hon-or comes, a pil-grim gray, To

bless the turf that wraps their clay; And free - dom shall a-while re-

bless the turf that wraps their clay; And free - dom shall a-while re-

bless the turf that wraps their clay; And free - dom shall a-while re-

pair, To dwell a weep-ing her - mit there! How sleep the brave, How sleep the brave.

pair, To dwell a weep-ing her - mit there! How sleep the brave, How sleep the brave.

pair, To dwell a weep-ing her - mit there! How sleep the brave, How sleep the brave.

OUR HOMES

HOME AGAIN!

Marshall S. Pike.

Marshall S. Pike.

1st and 2d Soprano.

1. Home a - gain, home a - gain, From a for - eign shore! And
2. Hap - py hearts, hap - py hearts, With mine have laughed in glee, And
3. Mu - sic sweet, mu - sic soft, Lin - gers round the place, And

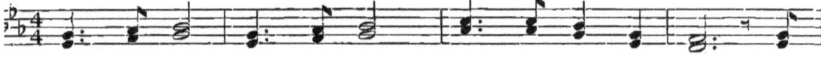

Alto-Tenor.

1. Home a - gain, home a - gain, From a for - eign shore! And
2. Hap - py hearts, hap - py hearts, With mine have laughed in glee, And
3. Mu - sic sweet, mu - sic soft, Lin - gers round the place, And

Tenor and Bass.

1. Home a - gain, home a - gain, From a for - eign shore! And
2. Hap - py hearts, hap - py hearts, With mine have laughed in glee, And
3. Mu - sic sweet, mu - sic soft, Lin - gers round the place, And

oh, it fills my soul with joy, To meet my friends once more.
oh, the friends I loved in youth, Seem hap - pi - er to me;
oh, I feel the child-hood charm That time can - not ef - face.

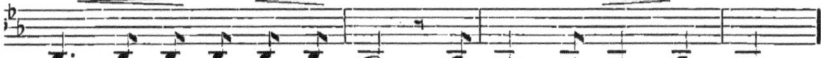

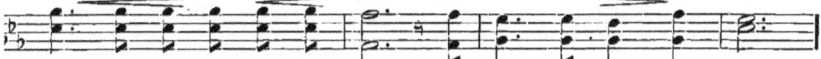

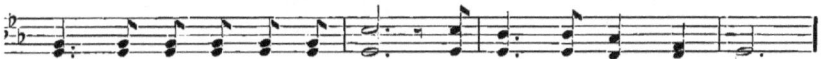

oh, it fills my soul with joy, To meet my friends once more.
oh, the friends I loved in youth, Seem hap - pi - er to me;
oh, I feel the child-hood charm That time can - not ef - face.

oh, it fills my soul with joy, To meet my friends once more.
oh, the friends I loved in youth, Seem hap - pi - er to me;
oh, I feel the child-hood charm That time can - not ef - face.

HOME AGAIN.

Here I dropped the part - ing tear, To cross the o - cean's foam,
And if my guide should be the fate, Which bids me long - er roam,
Then give me but my home - stead roof, I'll ask no pal - ace dome,

Here I dropped the part - ing tear, To cross the o - cean's foam,
And if my guide should be the fate, Which bids me long - er roam,
Then give me but my home - stead roof, I'll ask no pal - ace dome,

Here I dropped the part - ing tear, To cross the o - cean's foam,
And if my guide should be the fate, Which bids me long - er roam,
Then give me but my home - stead roof, I'll ask no pal - ace dome,

But now I'm once a - gain with those Who kind - ly greet me home.
But death a - lone can break the tie That binds my heart to home.
For I can live a hap - py life With those I love at home.

But now I'm once a - gain with those Who kind - ly greet me home.
But death a - lone can break the tie That binds my heart to home.
For I can live a hap - py life With those I love at home.

But now I'm once a - gain with those Who kind - ly greet me home.
But death a - lone can break the tie That binds my heart to home.
For I can live a hap - py life With those I love at home.

Home a - gain, home a - gain, From a for - eign shore! And

Home a - gain, home a - gain, From a for - eign shore! And

Home a - gain, home a - gain, From a for - eign shore! And

oh, it fills my soul with joy, To meet my friends once more.

oh, it fills my soul with joy, To meet my friends once more.

oh, it fills my soul with joy, To meet my friends once more.

AROUND THE HEARTH.

George Howland.

Scotch Air
(Air "Old Lang Syne.")

Andante.

1st and 2d Soprano.

1. What - ev - er be our earth - ly lot, Wher - ev - er we may roam, Still
2. When win - ter, com - ing in its wrath, Pil'd high the drift - ing snow, Safe
3. When wea - ried with our ea - ger chase, Thro' many a tan - gled path, How
4. And bright - er with the pass - ing years Seems child - hood's sweet em - ploy, And

Alto-Tenor.

1. What - ev - er be our earth - ly lot, Wher - ev - er we may roam, Still
2. When win - ter, com - ing in its wrath, Pil'd high the drift - ing snow, Safe
3. When wea - ried with our ea - ger chase, Thro' many a tan - gled path, How
4. And bright - er with the pass - ing years Seems child - hood's sweet em - ploy, And

Tenor and Bass.

1. What - ev - er be our earth - ly lot, Wher - ev - er we may roam, Still
2. When win - ter, com - ing in its wrath, Pil'd high the drift - ing snow, Safe
3. When wea - ried with our ea - ger chase, Thro' many a tan - gled path, How
4. And bright - er with the pass - ing years Seems child - hood's sweet em - ploy, And

to our hearts the bright - est spot Is round the hearth at home, The
clus - ter'd round the cheer - ful hearth, We watch'd the fire - light glow; Nor
sweet the dear ac - cus - tom'd place, To take a - round the hearth! And
ev - er sweet - er still ap - pears Each well - re - mem - ber'd joy, A -

to our hearts the bright - est spot Is round the hearth at home, The
clus - ter'd round the cheer - ful hearth, We watch'd the fire - light glow; Nor
sweet the dear ac - cus - tom'd place, To take a - round the hearth! And
ev - er sweet - er still ap - pears Each well - re - mem - ber'd joy, A -

to our hearts the bright - est spot Is round the hearth at home, The
clus - ter'd round the cheer - ful hearth, We watch'd the fire - light glow; Nor
sweet the dear ac - cus - tom'd place, To take a - round the hearth! And
ev - er sweet - er still ap - pears Each well - re - mem - ber'd joy, A -

cres.   *f*

home   that wel - comed   us   at   birth, The hearth   by which   we   sat;   No
bright - er seem'd   the   rud - dy flames Than did   our hearts, the   while A
still   when by   our   toil   and care   We   feel our - selves op - press'd, Our
round   the cheer - ful hearth at home, Where we   in child - hood   sat;   No

cres.   *f*

home   that wel - comed   us   at   birth, The hearth   by which   we   sat;   No
bright - er seem'd   the   rud - dy flames Than did   our hearts, the   while A
still   when by   our   toil   and care   We   feel our - selves op - press'd, Our
round   the cheer - ful hearth at home, Where we   in child - hood   sat;   No

cres.   *f*

home   that wel - comed   us   at   birth, The hearth   by which   we   sat;   No
bright - er seem'd   the   rud - dy flames Than did   our hearts, the   while A
still   when by   our   toil   and care   We   feel our - selves op - press'd, Our
round   the cheer - ful hearth at home, Where we   in child - hood   sat;   No

cres.   *f*

dim. e rall.

oth -   er   spot   on   all   the   earth Will ev - er   be   like that.
lov - ing moth - er breath'd our names With sweet ap - prov - ing smile.
thoughts for ev - er   clus - ter there, And there a - lone find rest.
oth -   er   spot, wher - e'er   we roam, Will ev - er   be   like that.

dim. e rall.

oth -   er   spot   on   all   the   earth Will ev - er   be   like that.
lov - ing moth - er breath'd our names With sweet ap - prov - ing smile.
thoughts for ev - er   clus - ter there, And there a - lone find rest.
oth -   er   spot, wher - e'er   we roam, Will ev - er   be   like that.

dim. e rall.

oth -   er   spot   on   all   the   earth Will ev - er   be   like that.
lov - ing moth - er breath'd our names With sweet ap - prov - ing smile.
thoughts for ev - er   clus - ter there, And there a - lone find rest.
oth -   er   spot, wher - e'er   we roam, Will ev - er   be   like that.

dim. e rall.

HOME, SWEET HOME.

John Howard Payne (1792 — 1852).

Sicilian Air.

1st and 2d Soprano.

1. 'Mid pleas-ures and pal - a - ces, tho' we may roam, Be it ev - er so hum - ble, there's
2. I gaze on the moon as I tread the drear wild, And feel that my moth - er now
3. An ex - ile from home, splen-dor daz - zles in vain; O give me my low - ly thatch'd

Alto-Tenor.

1. 'Mid pleas-ures and pal - a - ces tho' we may roam, Be it ev - er so hum - ble there's
2. I gaze on the moon as I tread the drear wild, And feel that my moth - er now
3. An ex - ile from home, splen-dor daz - zles in vain; Oh, give me my low - ly thatch'd

Tenor and Bass.

1. 'Mid pleas-ures and pal - a - ces tho' we may roam, Be it ev - er so hum - ble there's
2. I gaze on the moon as I tread the drear wild, And feel that my moth - er now
3. An ex - ile from home, splen-dor daz - zles in vain, Oh, give me my low - ly thatch'd

no place like home; A charm from the skies seems to hal - low us
thinks of her child, As she looks on that moon from our own cot - tage
cot - tage a - gain, The birds sing - ing gai - ly, that came at my

no place like home; A charm from the skies seems to hal - low us
thinks of her child, As she looks on that moon from our own cot - tage
cot - tage a - gain, The birds sing - ing gai - ly, that came at my

no place like home; A charm from the skies seems to hal - low us
thinks of her child, As she looks on that moon from our own cot - tage
cot - tage a - gain, The birds sing - ing gai - ly, that came at my

there,   Which, seek thro' the world, is ne'er met with else - where.   Home, home,
door,   'Mid the wood - bine whose fra - grance shall cheer me no more.   Home, home,
call;   Give me them, and that peace of mind, dear - er than all.   Home, home,

there,   Which, seek thro' the world, is ne'er met with else - where,   Home, home,
door,   'Mid the wood - bine whose fra - grance shall cheer me no more.   Home, home,
call;   Give me them, and that peace of mind, dear - er than all.   Home, home,

there,   Which, seek thro' the world, is ne'er met with else - where,   Home, home,
door,   Mid' the wood - bine whose fra - grance shall cheer me no more.   Home, home,
call;   Give me them, and that peace of mind, dear - er than all.   Home, home,

sweet, sweet home, Be it ev - er so hum - ble, there's no place like home.

sweet, sweet home, Be it ev - er so hum - ble, there's no place like home.

sweet, sweet home, Be it ev - er so hum - ble, there's no place like home.

OLD FOLKS AT HOME.

STEPHEN COLLINS FOSTER.

STEPHEN COLLINS FOSTER.

1. Way down up - on de Swa - nee rib - ber, Far, far a - way,
2. All round de lit - tle farm I wan-der'd When I was young;
3. One lit - tle hut a - mong de bush - es, One dat I love,

Dere's wha' my heart is turn - ing eb - er, Dere's wha' de old folks stay.
Den man - y hap - py days I squan-der'd, Man - y de songs I sung.
Still sad - ly to my mem -'ry rush - es, No mat - ter where I rove.

All up and down de whole cre - a - tion, Sad - ly I roam,
When I was play - ing wid my brud - der, Hap - py was I;
When will I see de bees a - hum - ming, All round de comb?

Still long-ing for de old plan-ta-tion, And for de old folks at home.
Oh, take me to my kind old mud-der, Dere let me live and die.
When will I hear de ban-jo tum-ming, Down in my good old home?

CHORUS.
1ST AND 2D SOPRANO.

All de world am sad and drear-y, Eb-'ry where I roam;

ALTO-TENOR.

All de world am sad and drear-y, Eb-'ry where I roam;

TENOR AND BASS.

All de world am sad and drear-y, Eb-'ry where I roam;

Oh, dark-ies, how my heart grows wea-ry, Far from de old folks at home.

Oh, dark-ies, how my heart grows wea-ry, Far from de old folks at home.

Oh, dark-ies, how my heart grows wea-ry, Far from de old folks at home.

W. T. WRIGHTON.

1ST AND 2D SOPRANO.

1. The dear - est spot of earth to me Is home, sweet home: The
2. I've taught my heart the way to prize My home, sweet home; I've

ALTO-TENOR.

1. The dear - est spot of earth to me Is home, sweet home; The
2. I've taught my heart the way to prize My home, sweet home; I've

TENOR AND BASS.

1. The dear - est spot of earth to me Is home, sweet home; The
2. I've taught my heart the way to prize My home, sweet home; I've

fair - y land I've longed to see Is home, sweet home.
learned to look with lov - er's eyes On home, sweet home.

fair - y land I've longed to see Is home, sweet home.
learned to look with lov - er's eyes On home, sweet home.

fair - y land I've longed to see Is home, sweet home.
learned to look with lov - er's eyes On home, sweet home.

There how charmed the sense of hear - ing, There where hearts are
There where vows are tru - ly plight - ed, There where hearts are

There how charmed the sense of hear - ing, There where hearts are
There where vows are tru - ly plight - ed, There where hearts are

There how charmed the sense of hear - ing, There where hearts are
There where vows are tru - ly plight - ed, There where hearts are

so en - dear - ing, All the world is not so cheer - ing, As
so u - ni - ted, All the world be - sides I've slight - ed, For

so en - dear - ing, All the world is not so cheer - ing, As
so u - ni - ted, All the world be - sides I've slight - ed, For

so en - dear - ing, All the world is not so cheer - ing, As
so u - ni - ted, 'All the world be - sides I've slight - ed, For

home, sweet home. The dear-est spot of earth to me Is home, sweet

home, sweet home. The dear-est spot of earth to me Is home, sweet

home, sweet home. The dear-est spot of earth to me Is home, sweet

home; The fair-y land I've longed to see Is home, sweet home.

home; The fair-y land I've longed to see Is home, sweet home.

home; The fair-y land I've longed to see Is home, sweet home.

HYMNS OF PATRIOTISM

ANGEL OF PEACE.

Written for the National Peace Festival.

Oliver Wendell Holmes (1809—1894.)

Matthias Keller.

1st and 2d Soprano.

1. An - gel of Peace, thou hast wan - dered too long! Spread thy white wings to the
2. Broth-ers we meet, on this al - tar of thine Ming - ling the gifts we have
3. An - gels of Beth - le - hem, an - swer the strain! Hark! a new birth - song is

Alto—Tenor.

1. An - gel of Peace, thou hast wan - dered too long! Spread thy white wings to the
2. Broth-ers we meet, on this al - tar of thine Ming - ling the gifts we have
3. An - gels of Beth - le - hem, an - swer the strain! Hark! a new birth - song is

Tenor and Bass.

1. An - gel of Peace, thou hast wan - dered too long! Spread thy white wings to the
2. Broth-ers we meet, on this al - tar of thine Ming - ling the gifts we have
3. An - gels of Beth - le - hem, an - swer the strain! Hark! a new birth - song is

Maestoso. ♩ =76.

sun - shine of love! Come while our voi - ces are blend - ed in song,
gath - ered for thee. Sweet with the o - dors of myr - tle and pine,
fill - ing the sky! Loud as the storm - wind that tum - bles the main,

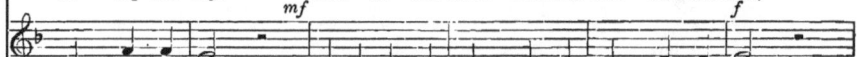

sun - shine of love! Come while our voi - ces are blend - ed in song,
gath - ered for thee. Sweet with the o - dors of myr - tle and pine,
fill - ing the sky! Loud as the storm - wind that tum - bles the main,

sun - shine of love! Come while our voi - ces are blend - ed in song,
gath - ered for thee. ·Sweet with the o - dors of myr - tle and pine,
fill - ing the sky! Loud as the storm - wind that tum - bles the main,

Fly   to   our ark   like   the storm - beat - en dove!   Fly   to our ark   on the
Breeze   of   the prai - rie and breath of   the sea,   Mea - dow and moun-tain and
Bid   the full breath of   the or - gan re-ply,   Let   the loud tem - pest of

Fly   to   our ark   like   the storm - beat - en dove!   Fly   to our ark   on the
Breeze   of   the prai - rie and breath of   the sea,   Mea - dow and moun-tain and
Bid   the full breath of   the or - gan re-ply,   Let   the loud tem - pest of

Fly   to   our ark   like   the storm - beat - en dove!   Fly   to our ark   on the
Breeze   of   the prai - rie and breath of   the sea,   Mea - dow and moun-tain and
Bid   the full breath of   the or - gan re-ply,   Let   the loud tem - pest of

wings   of   the dove, —   Speed o'er the far - sound-ing bil - lows of song,
for -   est and sea!   Sweet is   the fra - grance of myr - tle   and pine,
voi -   ces re-ply, —   Roll its long surge like the earth - shak-ing main!

wings   of   the dove, —   Speed o'er the far - sound-ing bil - lows of song,
for -   est and sea!   Sweet is   the fra - grance of myr - tle   and pine,
voi -   ces re-ply, —   Roll its long surge like the earth - shak-ing main!

wings   of   the dove, —   Speed o'er the far - sound-ing bil - lows of song,
for -   est and sea!   Sweet is   the fra - grance of myr - tle   and pine,
voi -   ces re-ply, —   Roll its long surge like the earth - shak-ing main!

Crowned with thine o - live - leaf gar - land of love,— An - gel of
Sweet - er the in - cense we of - fer to thee, Broth - ers once
Swell the vast song till it mounts to the sky!— An - gels of

Crowned with thine o - live - leaf gar - land of love,— An - gel of
Sweet - er the in - cense we of - fer to thee, Broth - ers once
Swell the vast song till it mounts to the sky!— An - gels of

Crowned with thine o - live - leaf gar - land of love,— An - gel of
Sweet - er the in - cense we of - fer to thee, Broth - ers once
Swell the vast song till it mounts to the sky!— An - gels of

Peace, thou hast wait - ed too long!
more round this al - tar of thine!
Beth - le - hem, ech - o the strain!

Peace, thou hast wait - ed too long!
more round this al - tar of thine!
Beth - le - hem, ech - o the strain!

Peace, thou hast wait - ed too long!
more round this al - tar of thine!
Beth - le - hem, ech - o the strain!

A MIGHTY FORTRESS IS OUR GOD.

"EINE FESTE BURG." MARTIN LUTHER, 1529.

1ST AND 2D SOPRANO.

1. A might-y for-tress is our God, A bul-wark nev-er fail - ing; Our
2. Did we in our own strength confide, Our striv-ing would be los - ing, Were
3. And tho' this world with dev-ils filled, Should threaten to un-do .... us, We
4. That word a - bove all earth-ly powers—No thanks to them-a - bid - eth, The

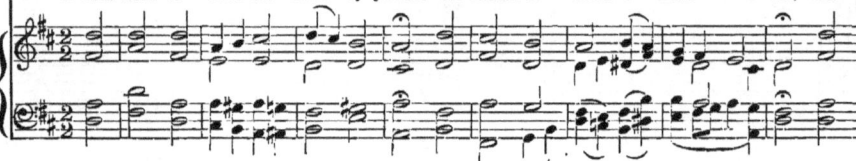

ALTO-TENOR.

1. A might-y for-tress is our God, A bul-wark nev-er fail - ing; Our
2. Did we in our own strength con-fide, Our striv-ing would be los - ing, Were
3. And tho' this world with dev-ils filled, Should threaten to un-do .... us, We
4. That word a - bove all earth-ly powers—No thanks to them-a - bid - eth, The

TENOR AND BASS.

1. A might-y for-tress is onr God, A bul-wark nev-er fail - ing; Our
2. Did we in our own strength con-tide, Our striv-ing would be los - ing, Were
3. And tho' this world with dev-ils filled, Should threaten to un-do .... us, We
4. That word a - bove all earth-ly powers—No thanks to them-a - bid - eth, The

help-er He a - mid the flood Of mor-tal ills pre - vail - ing. For
not the right man on our side, The man of God's own choos - ing. Dost
will not fear, for God hath willed His truth to tri - umph through .... us. The
spir-it and the gifts are ours, Thro' Him who with us sid - - eth. Let

help-er He a - mid the flood Of mor-tal ills pre - vail - ing. For
not the right man on our side, The man of God's own choos - ing. Dost
will not fear, for God hath willed His truth to tri - umph through .... us. The
spir-it and the gifts are ours, Thro' Him who with us sid - - eth. Let

help-er He a - mid the flood Of mor-tal ills pre - vail - ing. For
not the right man on our side, The man of God's own choos - ing. Dost
will not fear, for God hath willed His truth to tri - umph through .... us. The
spir-it and the gifts are ours, Thro' Him who with us sid - - eth. Let

still our an-cient foe Doth seek to work us woe, His craft and power are
ask who that may be? Christ Je-sus, it is He, Lord Sa - ba - oth His
Prince of Dark-ness grim, We trem-ble not for him, His rage we can en -
goods and kin-dred go, This mor-tal life al - so; The bod-y they may

still our an-cient foe Doth seek to work us woe, His craft and power are
ask who that may be? Christ Je-sus, it is He, Lord Sa - ba - oth His
Prince of Dark-ness grim, We trem-ble not for him, His rage we can en -
goods and kin-dred go, This mor-tal life al - so; The bod-y they may

still our an-cient foe Doth seek to work us woe, His craft and power are
ask who that may be? Christ Je-sus, it is He, Lord Sa - ba - oth His
Prince of Dark-ness grim, We trem-ble not for him, His rage we can en -
goods and kin-dred go, This mor-tal life al - so; The bod-y they may

great, And, armed with cru - el hate, On earth is not his e - - qual.
name, From age to age the same, And He must win the bat - - tle.
dure, For lo! his doom is sure; One lit - tle word shall fell - - him.
kill, God's truth a - bid - eth still, His king - dom is for ev - - er.

great, And, armed with cru - el hate, On earth is not his e - - qual.
name, From age to age the same, And He must win the bat - - tle.
dure, For lo! his doom is sure; One lit - tle word shall fell - - him.
kill, God's truth a - bid - eth still, His king - dom is for ev - - er.

great, And, armed with cru - el hate, On earth is not his e - - qual.
name, From age to age the same, And He must win the bat - - tle.
dure, For lo! his doom is sure; One lit - tle word shall fell - - him.
kill, God's truth a - bid - eth still, His king - dom is for ev - - er.

BATTLE HYMN OF THE REPUBLIC.

Julia Ward Howe.

Air "John Brown's Body."

mf

1. Mine eyes have seen the glo-ry of the
2. I have seen Him in the watch-fires of a
3. I have read a fier-y gos-pel writ in
4. He has sounded forth the trum-pet that shall
5. In the beau-ty of the lil-ies Christ was

com-ing of the Lord; He is tramp-ling out the vin-tage where the
'hun-dred cir-cling camps; They have build-ed Him an al-tar in the
bur-nished rows of steel, "As ye deal with my con-tem-ners, so with
nev-er sound re-treat, He is sift-ing out the hearts of men be-
born a-cross the sea, With a glo-ry in His bo-som that trans-

grapes of wrath are stored; He hath loos'd the fate-ful light-ning of His
eve-ning dews and damps; I can read His right-eous sen-tence in the
you My grace shall deal; Let the he-ro born of wo-man crush the
fore His judg-ment seat; O, be swift, my soul, to an-swer Him, be
fig-ures you and me; As He died to make men ho-ly, let us

ter-ri-ble swift sword; His truth is march-ing on.
dim and flar-ing lamps; His day is march-ing on.
ser-pent with his heel, Since God is march-ing on.
ju-bi-lant, my feet! Our God is march-ing on.
die to make men free, While God is march-ing on.

Used by permission.

GLORY, GLORY HALLELUJAH.

1 ‖: John Brown's body lies a mould'ring in the grave, :‖
    His soul is marching on.

2 ‖: The stars of Heaven are looking kindly down, :‖
    On the grave of old John Brown.

3 He's gone to be a soldier in the army of the Lord! :‖
    His soul is marching on.

4 ‖: John Brown's knapsack is strapped upon his back, :‖:
    His soul is marching on.

5 ‖: His pet lambs will meet him on the way, :‖
    And they'll go marching on.

BLEST OF GOD! THE GOD OF NATIONS.

COLUMBIA'S JUBILEE.

GRANVILLE B. PUTNAM.

Maestoso.

J. ELIOT TROWBRIDGE.

1. Blest of God! the God of Na - - tions, Hail! Co - lum - bia; Hail to thee! . . .
2. Hon - or pay the dauntless voy - - ager From the shores of proud Cas - tile, ...

1. Blest of God! the God of Na - - tions, Hail! Co - lum - bia; Hail to thee! . . .
2. Hon - or pay the daunt-less voy - - ager From the shores of proud Cas - tile, . . .

Let the lips of hap - py mil - lions Sound the notes of Ju - bi - lee.
First to sail the west - ern wa - - ters, On - ward urged by fer - vent zeal.

Raise a - loft the star - ry ban - ner, Proud-ly may its lov'd folds wave,
God's own er - rand led those white wings To this wait - ing sun - set land,

(BASS. *ad lib.*)

Proud - ly may its lov'd folds wave,
To this wait - ing sun - set land,

TUTTI.

Tell-ing all thy fade-less glo - - ry, And the val - or of thy brave,
Where Co-lum-bus breath'd his prais - - es, Kneel-ing on the spray-wet sand,

Tell-ing all thy fade-less glo - - ry, And the val - or of thy brave,
Where Co-lum-bus breath'd his prais - - es, Kneel-ing on the spray-wet sand,

Tell-ing all thy fade-less glo - ry, And the val - or of thy brave.
Where Co-lum-bus breath'd his prais - es, Kneel-ing on the spray-wet sand.

Tell-ing all thy fade-less glo - ry, And the val - or of thy brave.
Where Co-lum-bus breath'd his prais - es, Kneel-ing on the spray-wet sand.

Interlude between 1st and 2d also 2d and 3d Verses.

ril.

3. Faith, a pil - grim, rock'd thy cra - - - dle By the sul - len win - try sea, ...
4. Lo! what fu - ture vic - t'ries wait thee On the blood-less fields of peace, . . .

3. Faith, a pil - grim, rock'd thy cra - - - dle By the sul - len win - t'ry sea, . . .
4. Lo! what fu - ture vic - t'ries wait thee On the blood-less fields of peace, . . .

DUET. 1ST AND 2D SOPRANO.

And the arm of loy - al he - roes From each foe de - fend - ed thee.
Sci - ence, Learn - ing, Truth, thine al - lies, Nev - er shall thy tri - umph cease.

2D SOPRANOS AND ALTOS IN UNISON.

Fer - tile plains and teem - ing wa - ters Fill thy lap with wealth un - told,
One in heart, with voi - ces blend - ing, North and South, your trib - ute raise!
(BASS. ad lib.)

Fill thy lap with wealth un - told,
North and South, your trib - ute raise!

TUTTI.

But thy chil-dren's fond de - vo - tion Far outweighs thy treasured gold,
Sound a-loud the might - y cho - rus, Shout! O shout! Co-lum-bia's praise,

But thy chil-dren's fond de - vo - tion Far outweighs thy treas-ured gold,
Sound a-loud the might - y cho - rus, Shout! O shout! Co-lum-bia's praise,

But thy chil-dren's fond de - vo - tion Far outweighs thy treas-ured gold.
Sound a-loud the might - y cho - rus, Shout! O shout! Co-lum-bia's praise.

But thy chil-dren's fond de - vo - tion Far out-weighs thy treas-ured gold.
Sound a-loud the might - y cho - rus, Shout! O shout! Co-lum-bia's praise.

Interlude between 3d and 4th Verses.

ff

ril.

COLUMBIA.

GIVE THANKS TO GOD.

(*A National Hymn of Praise.*)

Words and Music by Gen. LUTHER STEPHENSON.

Allegro.

1st AND 2D SOPRANO.

1. Give thanks to God with loud ac-claim For bless-ings to our Na-tion; Sing
2. Give thanks to God for Free-dom's rays, Co-lum-bia's path-way light-ing; A
3. Give thanks to God for cease-less care, A par-ent's love ex-cell-ing; For

ALTO-TENOR.

1. Give thanks to God with loud ac-claim For bless-ings to our Na-tion; Sing
2. Give thanks to God for Free-dom's rays, Co-lum-bia's path-way light-ing; A
3. Give thanks to God for cease-less care, A par-ent's love ex-cell-ing; For

TENOR AND BASS.

1. Give thanks to God with loud ac-claim For bless-ings to our Na-tion; Sing
2. Give thanks to God for Free-dom's rays, Co-lum-bia's path-way light-ing; A
3. Give thanks to God for cease-less care, A par-ent's love ex-cell-ing; For

prais-es to His glo-rious Name, With hum-ble ad-o-ra-tion! Give
star of hope, though dark-est days To dis-tant climes be-night-ed! Give
gifts and good-ness ev-'ry-where, His con-stant guid-ance tell-ing! Give

prais-es to His glo-rious Name, With hum-ble ad-o-ra-tion! Give
star of hope, though dark-est days To dis-tant climes be-night-ed! Give
gifts and good-ness ev-'ry-where, His con-stant guid-ance tell-ing! Give

prais-es to His glo-rious Name, With hum-ble ad-o-ra-tion! Give
star of hope, though dark-est days To dis-tant climes be-night-ed! Give
gifts and good-ness ev-'ry-where, His con-stant guid-ance tell-ing! Give

thanks to God, who led our sires A - cross the storm - y o - cean, To
thanks to God, our songs em - ploy, For skies with beau - ty beam - ing; While
thanks to God for end - less grace, With earn - est sup - pli - ca - tions, To

thanks to God, who led our sires A - cross the storm - y o - cean, To
thanks to God, our songs em - ploy, For skies with beau - ty beam - ing; While
thanks to God for end - less grace, With earn - est sup - pli - ca - tions, To

thanks to God, who led our sires A - cross the storm - y o - cean, To
thanks to God, our songs em - ploy, For skies with beau - ty beam - ing; While
thanks to God for end - less grace, With earn - est sup - pli - ca - tions, To

light with love the al - tar fires Of Pa - tri - ot's de - vo - tion!
hills and val - leys shout for joy, With Na - ture's trib - utes teem - ing!
make our land His dwell - ing place, Thro' count - less gen - er - a - tions!

light with love the al - tar fires Of Pa - tri - ot's de - vo - tion!
hills and val - leys shout for joy, With Na - ture's trib - utes teem - ing!
make our land His dwell - ing place, Thro' count - less gen - er - a - tions!

light with love the al - tar fires Of Pa - tri - ot's de - vo - tion!
hills and val - leys shout for joy, With Na - ture's trib - utes teem - ing!
make our land His dwell - ing place, Thro' count - less gen - er - a - tions!

CHARLES WESLEY.

(FELICE GIARDINI, 1716-1796.)

1ST AND 2D SOPRANO.

1. Come, Thou Al - might - y King! Help us Thy name to sing,
2. Come, Thou all - gra - cious Lord, By heaven and earth a - dored,
3. Nev - er from us . . de - part; Rule Thou in ev - 'ry heart,

ALTO–TENOR.

1. Come, Thou Al - might - y King! Help us Thy name to sing,
2. Come, Thou all - gra - cious Lord, By heaven and earth a - dored,
3. Nev - er from us . . de - part; Rule Thou in ev - 'ry heart,

TENOR AND BASS.

1. Come, Thou Al - might - y King! Help us Thy name to sing,
2. Come, Thou all - gra - cious Lord, By heaven and earth a - dored,
3. Nev - er from us . . de - part; Rule Thou in ev - 'ry heart,

Help us to praise! Fa - ther, all - glo - ri - ous, O'er all vic -
Our prayer at - tend! Come, and Thy chil - dren bless; Give Thy good
Hence, ev - er - more, Thy sov - 'reign ma - jes - ty May we in

Help us to praise! Fa - ther, all - glo - ri - ous, O'er all vic -
Our prayer at - tend! Come, and Thy chil - dren bless; Give Thy good
Hence, ev - er - more, Thy sov - 'reign ma - jes - ty May we in

Help us to praise! Fa - ther, all - glo - ri - ous, O'er all vic -
Our prayer at - tend! Come, and Thy chil - dren bless; Give Thy good
Hence, ev - er - more, Thy sov - 'reign ma - jes - ty May we in

to - ri - ous,	Come and	reign	o - ver us,	An - cient	of	Days!
word	suc - cess;	Make Thine	own	ho - li - ness	On	us	de - scend.
glo - ry	see!	And	to	e - ter - ni - ty	Love	and	a - dore.

to - ri - ous,	Come and	reign	o - ver us,	An - cient	of	Days!
word	suc - cess;	Make Thine	own	ho - li - ness	On	us	de - scend.
glo - ry	see!	And	to	e - ter - ni - ty	Love	and	a - dore.

to - ri - ous,	Come and	reign	o - ver us,	An - cient	of	Days!
word	suc - cess;	Make Thine	own	ho - li - ness	On	us	de - scend.
glo - ry	see!	And	to	e - ter - ni - ty	Love	and	a - dore.

DEAR REFUGE, NEVER FAILING.

Rev. E. J. COLCORD.   B. MARTELL. Arr. by F. W.

1ST AND 2D SOPRANO.

1. Dear Ref - uge, nev - er fail - ing, In storms of war pre - vail - ing, O'er
2. When o'er our night of sor - row There dawned a bright - er mor - row, Then
3. For ev - er then, O Fa - ther, When shad - ows round us gath - er, Up -

ALTO-TENOR.

1. Dear Ref - uge, nev - er fail - ing, In storms of war pre - vail - ing, O'er
2. When o'er our night of sor - row There dawned a bright - er mor - row, Then
3. For ev - er then, O Fa - ther, When shad - ows round us gath - er, Up -

TENOR AND BASS.

1. Dear Ref - uge, nev - er fail - ing, In storms of war pre - vail - ing, O'er
2. When o'er our night of · sor - row There dawned a bright - er mor - row, Then
3. For ev - er then, O Fa - ther, When shad - ows round us gath - er, Up -

path - ways lone and wea - ry, Thro' shad - ows dark and drea - ry, Thy
thro' their tears the liv - ing Poured forth their glad thanks - giv - ing, To
on Thy love re - ly - ing, Our hearts with faith un - dy - ing, On

path - ways lone and wea. - ry, Thro' shad - ows dark and drea - ry, Thy
thro' their tears the liv - ing Poured forth their glad thanks - giv - ing, To
on Thy love re - ly - ing, Our hearts with faith un - dy - ing, On

path - ways lone and wea - ry, Thro' shad - ows dark and drea - ry, Thy
thro' their tears the liv - ing Poured forth their glad thanks - giv - ing, To
on Thy love re - ly - ing, Our hearts with faith un - dy - ing, On

ten - der love our na - tion led, And blessed the land where he - roes bled.
Thee whose lov - ing - kind - ness gave Sweet peace to dead and loy - al brave.
Thee shall call, O Sov - 'reign Will, To save our no - ble land from ill.

ten - der love our na - tion led, And blessed the land where he - roes bled.
Thee whose lov - ing - kind - ness gave Sweet peace to dead and loy - al brave.
Thee shall call, O Sov - 'reign Will, To save our no - ble land from ill.

ten - der love our na - tion led, And blessed the land where he - roes bled.
Thee whose lov - ing - kind - ness gave Sweet peace to dead and loy - al brave.
Thee shall call, O Sov - 'reign Will, To save our no - ble land from ill.

GOD OF OUR FATHERS.

PRAYER FOR THE REPUBLIC.

Rev. S. Wolcott, D.D.
1st and 2d Soprano.

H. P. Danks.
Arr. by J. Eliot Trowbridge.

mf

1. God of our Fa - thers, let Thy face Toward the Re - pub - lic ev - er be!
2. Un - to our Pres - i - dent im - part Sus - tain - ing trust, dis - cern - ing sight,
3. With - in our Con - gress let the fires Of pa - tri - ot - ic love a - bide.
4. Up - on our Judg - es let the seal Of Thy di - vine an - oint - ing be,

Alto—Tenor.
mf

1. God of our Fa - thers, let Thy face Toward the Re - pub - lic ev - er be!
2. Un - to our Pres - i - dent im - part Sus - tain - ing trust, dis - cern - ing sight,
3. With - in our Con - gress let the fires Of pa - tri - ot - ic love a - bide!
4. Up - on our Judg - es let the seal Of Thy di - vine an - oint - ing be,

Tenor and Bass.
mf

mf

mf

f

En - com-pass it with strength and grace, And law com-bine with lib - er - ty.
The hom-age of the loy - al heart, The stead-fast cour-age for the right.
Its coun-sels lead, its acts in - spire, And in the na - tion's halls pre - side.
The wis-dom calm, the right-eous zeal, The robes of truth and e - qui - ty.

f

En - com-pass it with strength and grace, And law com-bine with lib - er - ty.
The hom-age of the loy - al heart, The stead-fast cour-age for the right.
Its coun-sels lead, its acts in - spire, And in the na - tion's halls pre - side.
The wis-dom calm, the right-eous zeal, The robes of truth and e - qui - ty.

f

f

HENRY F. CHORLEY (1808–1872).　　　　　　　　　ALEXIS VON LVOFF (1799–1870).

1ST AND 2D SOPRANO.

1. God the All - ter - ri - ble! King, who or - dain - est Great winds Thy
2. God the All - mer - ci - ful! earth hath for - sak - en Thy ways of
3. God the All - righteous One! Man hath de - fied Thee; Yet to e -
4. God the All - wise! by the fire of Thy chas - tening Earth shall to

ALTO-TENOR.

1. God the All - ter - ri - ble! King, who or - dain - est Great winds Thy
2. God the All - mer - ci - ful! earth hath for - sak - en Thy ways of
3. God the All - righteous One! Man hath de - fied Thee; Yet to e -
4. God the All - wise! by the fire of Thy chas - tening Earth shall to

TENOR AND BASS.

1. God the All - ter - ri - ble! King, who or - dain - est Great winds Thy
2. God the All - mer - ci - ful! earth hath for - sak - en Thy ways of
3. God the All - righteous One! Man hath de - fied Thee; Yet to e -
4. God the All - wise! by the fire of Thy chas - tening Earth shall to

clar - ions, the light - nings Thy sword; Show forth Thy pi - ty on high where Thou
bless - ed - ness, slight - ed Thy word; Bid not Thy wrath in its ter - rors a -
ter - ni - ty stand - eth Thy word; False-hood and wrong shall not tar - ry be -
free - dom and truth be re - stored; Thro' the thick dark - ness Thy king - dom is

clar - ions, the light - nings Thy sword; Show forth Thy pi - ty on high where Thou
bless - ed - ness, slight - ed Thy word; Bid not Thy wrath in its ter - rors a -
ter - ni - ty stand - eth Thy word; False-hood and wrong shall not tar - ry be -
free - dom and truth be re - stored; Thro' the thick dark - ness Thy king - dom is

clar - ions, the light - nings Thy sword; Show forth Thy pi - ty on high where Thou
bless - ed - ness, slight - ed Thy word; Bid not Thy wrath in its ter - rors a -
ter - ni - ty stand - eth Thy word; False-hood and wrong shall not tar - ry be -
free - dom and truth be re - stored; Thro' the thick dark - ness Thy king - dom is

reign	- est;	Give	to	us	peace	in	our	time,	O	Lord!
wak	- en;	Give	to	us	peace	in	our	time,	O	Lord!
side	Thee;	Give	to	us	peace	in	our	time,	O	Lord!
has	- tening;	Thou	wilt	give	peace	in	Thy	time,	O	Lord!

(repeated for Alto-Tenor part)

reign	- est;	Give	to	us	peace	in	our	time,	O	Lord!
wak	- en;	Give	to	us	peace	in	our	time,	O	Lord!
side	Thee;	Give	to	us	peace	in	our	time,	O	Lord!
has	- tening;	Thou	wilt	give	peace	in	Thy	time,	O	Lord!

(repeated for Tenor and Bass part)

reign	- est;	Give	to	us	peace	in	our	time,	O	Lord!
wak	- en;	Give	to	us	peace	in	our	time,	O	Lord!
side	Thee;	Give	to	us	peace	in	our	time,	O	Lord!
has	- tening;	Thou	wilt	give	peace	in	Thy	time,	O	Lord!

GOD BLESS OUR NATIVE LAND.

Words and music by S. PARKMAN TUCKERMAN.

1ST AND 2D SOPRANO.

1. God bless our na - tive land, On this firm shore we stand,
2. Send us Thy truth and love, Guide us to look a - bove,
3. This hymn of praise we sing To God, the migh - ty King,

ALTO-TENOR.

1. God bless our na - tive land, On this firm shore we stand,
2. Send us Thy truth and love, Guide us to look a - bove,
3. This hymn of praise we sing To God, the migh - ty King,

TENOR AND BASS.

1. God bless our na - tive land, On this firm shore we stand,
2. Send us Thy truth and love, Guide us to look a - bove,
3. This hymn of praise we sing To God, the migh - ty King,

For Free - dom's rights. Let us a - rise in might, Dis - pel the shades of night,
For all we need. Show us the way to go, From Thee all mer - cies flow!
En - thron'd a - bove! May He our na - tion guide, From ev - 'ry dan - ger hide,

For Free - dom's rights. Let us a - rise in might, Dis - pel the shades of night,
For all we need. Show us the way to go, From Thee all mer - cies flow!
En - thron'd a - bove! May He our na - tion guide, From ev - 'ry dan - ger hide,

For Free - dom's rights. Let us a - rise in might, Dis - pel the shades of night,
For all we need. Show us the way to go, From Thee all mer - cies flow!
En - thron'd a - bove! May He our na - tion guide, From ev - 'ry dan - ger hide,

And ban - ish them for light And truth, we pray.
Teach us Thy Name to know, For this we pray.
And with us still a - bide To shield and bless! A - MEN.

And ban - ish them for light And truth, we pray.
Teach us Thy Name to know, For this we pray.
And with us still a - bide To shield and bless! A - MEN.

And ban - ish them for light And truth, we pray.
Teach us Thy Name to know, For this we pray.
And with us still a - bide To shield and bless! A - MEN.

1. God save our Un - ion! God save our land! From all dis - un - ion Keep heart and hand.
2. Fa - ther im - mor-tal, Our sen - ti - nel, Stand at the por - tal, Guard our land well;

True to our na - tion, True un - to Thee, Lord of cre - a - tion, Help us to be.
Bless us with rea - son, Peace to main - tain, Ban - ish all trea-son From our do - main.

True to our na - tion, True un - to Thee, Lord of cre - a - tion, Help us to be.
Bless us with rea - son, Peace to main - tain, Ban - ish all trea-son From our do - main.

True to our na - tion, True un - to Thee, Lord of cre - a - tion, Help us to be.
Bless us with rea - son, Peace to main - tain, Ban - ish all trea-son From our do - main.

MAY GOD PROTECT COLUMBIA.

A PATRIOTIC HYMN.

SOPRANO SOLO AND CHORUS.

Words and music by J. R. THOMAS.
Arr. by J. ELIOT TROWBRIDGE.

SOPRANO SOLO.

1. May God pro-tect Co-lum-bia, And grant she still may be The hal-low'd home of
2. May God pro-tect Co-lum-bia, Thro'out her wide do-main, From East to West, from
3. May God pro-tect Co-lum-bia, Our hope and our de-sire! And ev-'ry true and
4. May God pro-tect Co-lum-bia, When foes her peace as-sail! And guide the glo-rious

SOPRANO AND ALTO DUET.

Lib-er-ty, The glo-ry of the free! Still faith'-ful to the her-it-age Our
North to South, May peace and plen-ty reign; May jus-tice, truth, and hap-pi-ness Ex-
loy-al heart To wor-thy deeds in-spire. Where Learn-ing's light is ev-er free, And
ship of state Tri-umph-ant thro' the gale. And so our coun-try's flag shall wave Re-

fa-thers left of yore; A shin-ing light to all the world, Both now and ev-er-more. . .
tend o'er all the land, And u-ni-ver-sal broth-er-hood U-nite each heart and hand. . .
Ign'rance doom'd to fall, There may our flag for ev-er wave, Tri-umph-ant o-ver all! . . .
splen-dent as of yore, The em-blem of true Lib-er-ty, From shore to farthest shore. . .

1ST AND 2D SOPRANO.

Then long live dear Co - lum - bia, And may she ev - er be The

ALTO—TENOR.

Then long live dear Co - lum - bia, And may she ev - er be The

TENOR AND BASS.

Then long live dear Co - lum - bia, And may she ev - er be The

hal - low'd home of Lib - er - ty, The glo - ry of the free!

hal - low'd home of Lib - er - ty, The glo - ry of the free!

hal - low'd home of Lib - er - ty, The glo - ry of the free!

PRAISE YE THE FATHER.

TRIUMPHAL MARCH.

Charles Gounod (1818–1893).
Arr. by J. P. Weston.

ben - e - fits; Sing forth your prais - es,— Let ev - 'ry heart be joy - ful.

ben - e - fits;. Sing forth your prais - es,— Let ev - 'ry heart be joy - ful.

ben - e - fits; Sing forth your prais - es,— Let ev - 'ry heart be joy - ful.

ben - e - fits; Sing forth your prais - es,— Let ev - 'ry heart be joy - ful.

Praise ye . . the Fa - ther, Great Ru - ler, kind and mer - ci - ful!

Praise ye . . the Fa - ther, Great Ru - ler, kind and mer - ci - ful!

Praise ye . . the Fa - ther, Great Ru - ler, kind and mer - ci - ful!

Praise ye . . the Fa - ther, Great Ru - ler, kind and mer - ci - ful!

Praise .. be to Him! ... who hath shown His might-y pow'r. .. Let ev'-ry

All praise   to Him who hath shown His might-y pow'r. ...

All praise   to Him who hath shown His might-y pow'r. ...

All praise   to Him who hath shown His might-y pow'r. ...

voice. . . sound His praise . . with ex-ult-ing strains of glad - ness!

Sing forth   His praise with ex-ult-ing strains of glad - ness!

Sing forth   His praise, with ex-ult-ing strains of glad - ness!

Sing forth   His praise, with ex-ult-ing strains of glad - ness!

Great . . is the Lord! . . Let His name be prais'd for ev - er; Come ye

Oh, great is He! Let His name be prais'd for ev - er; Come ye

Oh, great is He! let His name be prais'd for ev - er; Come ye

Oh, great is He! let His name be prais'd for ev - er; Come ye

forth with your hearts at - tuned to sing; A - rise, and praise ye the Fa - ther!

forth with your hearts at - tuned to sing; A - rise, and praise ye the Fa - ther!

forth with your hearts at - tuned to sing; A - rise, and praise ye the Fa - ther!

forth with your hearts at - tuned to sing; A - rise, and praise ye the Fa - ther!

Glo - ry to the Fa - ther! To the great and might-y Ru - ler! Glo - ry to the

Glo - ry to the Fa - ther! To the great and might - y Ru - ler! Glo - ry to the

Glo - ry to the Fa - ther! To the great and might - y Ru - ler! Glo - ry to the

Glo - ry to the Fa - ther! To the great and might - y Ru - ler! Glo - ry to the

Fa - ther, Who a - lone hath the pow'r to save! Loud - ly let the

Fa - ther, Who a - lone hath the pow'r to save! Loud - ly let the

Fa - ther, Who a - lone hath the pow'r to save, Who can save! Loud - ly let the

Fa - ther, Who a - lone hath the pow'r to save, Who can save! Loud - ly let the cho - rus swell! Loud - ly let the tune - ful an - them ring! Love and joy be now in

cho - rus swell! Loud - ly let the tune - ful an - them ring! Love and joy be now in

cho - rus swell! Loud - ly let the tune - ful an - them ring! Love and joy be now in

cho - rus swell! Loud - ly let the tune - ful an - them ring! Love and joy be now in

ev - 'ry thankful heart! O, praise ye the Lord! praise now the Lord!

ev - 'ry thankful heart! O, praise ye the Lord! praise now the Lord!

ev - 'ry thankful heart! O, praise ye the Lord! praise now the Lord!

ev - 'ry thankful heart! O, praise ye the Lord! praise now the Lord!

OLD HUNDRED.

Isaac Watts.   L. Bourgeois in the Genevan Psalter, 1551.

1st and 2d Soprano.

1. From all that dwell be - low the skies, Let the Cre - a - tor's praise a - rise;
2. E - ter - nal are Thy mer - cies, Lord; E - ter - nal truth at - tends Thy word;

Alto-Tenor.

1. From all that dwell be - low the skies, Let the Cre - a - tor's praise a - rise;
2. E - ter - nal are Thy mer - cies, Lord; E - ter - nal truth at - tends Thy word;

Tenor and Bass.

1. From all that dwell be - low the skies, Let the Cre - a - tor's praise a - rise;
2. E - ter - nal are Thy mer - cies, Lord; E - ter - nal truth at - tends Thy word;

Let the Re - deem - er's name be sung Thro' ev - 'ry land, by ev - 'ry tongue.
Thy praise shall sound from shore to shore, Till suns shall rise and set no more.

Let the Re - deem - er's name be sung Thro' ev - 'ry land, by ev - 'ry tongue.
Thy praise shall sound from shore to shore, Till suns shall rise and set no more.

Let the Re - deem - er's name be sung Thro' ev - 'ry land, by ev - 'ry tongue.
Thy praise shall sound from shore to shore, Till suns shall rise and set no more.

SOUND FORTH AGAIN THE NATION'S VOICE.

Thomas Wentworth Higginson.   C. Crozat Converse.

Choral style and march time.

1ST AND 2D SOPRANO.

1. Sound forth a - gain the na - tion's voice To God, who ruled the an - cient days;
2. The sea that girds our land with blue, The winds that make it wave with wheat,
3. Strike down the bars of pride and scorn; Lead up the low - ly, shield the pure,
4. Un - til the peo - ple all shall find, 'Mid strife of votes, 'mid jar of tongue,
5. Wher - e'er our star - ry flag may wave, Far as our na - tion's rule may span,

ALTO-TENOR.

1. Sound forth a - gain the na - tion's voice To God, who ruled the an - cient days;
2. The sea that girds our land with blue, The winds that make it wave with wheat,
3. Strike down the bars of pride and scorn; Lead up the low - ly, shield the pure,
4. Un - til the peo - ple all shall find, 'Mid strife of votes, 'mid jar of tongue,
5. Wher - e'er our star - ry flag may wave, Far as our na - tion's rule may span,

TENOR AND BASS.

His power will make our hearts re - joice, Can we but tread our fa - thers' ways.
Are wit - ness - es for ev - er true, That strength and free - dom here shall meet.
And be a no - bler na - tion born, To dare, to shel - ter, to en - dure.
The peace that glad - dens all man - kind, The love that keeps us ev - er young.
Let our firm pur - pose, true and brave, Bind all to God, and man with man.

His power will make our hearts re - joice, Can we but tread our fa - thers' ways.
Are wit - ness - es for ev - er true, That strength and free - dom here shall meet.
And be a no - bler na - tion born, To dare, to shel - ter, to en - dure.
The peace that glad - dens all man - kind, The love that keeps us ev - er young.
Let our firm pur - pose, true and brave, Bind all to God, and man with man.

UNION AND LIBERTY.

NATIONAL ANTHEM.

Oliver Wendell Holmes (1809–1894).　　　　　　　　　　　F. Boott.

Tempo di Marcia.

1st and 2d Soprano.

Flag of the he-roes who left us their glo-ry, Borne thro' their battle-fields' thun-der and flame,

Alto–Tenor

Flag of the he-roes who left us their glo-ry, Borne thro' their battle-fields' thun-der and flame,

Tenor and Bass.

Flag of the he-roes who left us their glo-ry, Borne thro' their battle-fields' thun-der and flame,

Bla-zoned in song and il-lum-ined in sto-ry, Wave o'er us all who in-her-it their fame!

Bla-zoned in song and il-lum-ined in sto-ry, Wave o'er us all who in-her-it their fame!

Bla-zoned in song and il-lum-ined in sto-ry, Wave o'er us all who in-her-it their fame!

The Hymn can be sung as a Solo, the chorus repeating from 𝄋.

Up with the ban-ner bright, Shining with star - ry light, Spread its fair emblems from mountain to shore,

Up with the ban-ner bright, Shining with star - ry light, Spread its fair emblems from mountain to shore,

Up with the ban-ner bright, Shining with star - ry light, Spread its fair emblems from mountain to shore,

While thro' the sounding sky Loud rings the Na-tion's cry, Un - ion and lib - er - ty! One ev - er-more!

While thro' the sounding sky Loud rings, . . Un - ion and lib - er - ty! One ev - er-more!

Loud rings, Un - ion and lib - er - ty! One ev - er-more!

* If but one bass, sing the the lower notes.

UNION AND LIBERTY.

2. Lord of the U - ni - verse! Shield us and guide us,

2. Lord of the U - ni - verse! Shield us and guide us,

2. Lord of the U - ni - verse! Shield us and guide us,

Trust - ing Thee al - ways, thro' shad - ow and sun. Thou hast u - nit - ed us;

Trust - ing Thee al - ways, thro' shad - ow and sun. Thou hast u - nit - ed us;

Trust - ing Thee al - ways, thro' shad - ow and sun. Thou hast u - nit - ed us;

D.S. al fine.

Who shall di - vide us? Keep us, O keep us the Ma - ny in One!

Who shall di - vide us? Keep us, O keep us the Ma - ny in One!

Who shall di - vide us? Keep us, O keep us the Ma - ny in One!

Who shall di - vide us? Keep us, O keep us the Ma - ny in One!

D.S. al fine.

NATIONAL DAYS.

MOUNT VERNON BELLS.

M. B. C. Slade.   Stephen Collins Foster (1826–1864).

Vessels and steamers going up and down the Potomac, toll their bells in passing Mount Vernon; a perpetual tribute of respect to the memory of Washington.

Poco lento.

1st and 2d Soprano.

1. Where Po - to-mac's stream is flow - ing Vir - gin - ia's bor - der through;
2. Long a - go the war - rior slum - bered; Our coun - try's Fa - ther slept;
3. Sail, oh ships, a - cross the bil - lows! And bear the sto - ry far,

Alto-Tenor.

1. Where Po - to-mac's stream is flow - ing Vir - gin - ia's bor - der through;
2. Long a - go the war - rior slum - bered; Our coun - try's Fa - ther slept;
3. Sail, oh ships, a - cross the bil - lows! And bear the sto - ry far,

Tenor and Bass.

1. Where Po - to-mac's stream is flow - ing Vir - gin - ia's bor - der through;
2. Long a - go the war - rior slum - bered; Our coun - try's Fa - ther slept;
3. Sail, oh ships, a - cross the bil - lows! And bear the sto - ry far,

Where the white-sailed ships are go - ing, Sail - ing to the o - cean blue;
Long, a - mong the an - gels num - bered, They the he - ro-soul have kept.
How he sleeps be-neath the wil - lows, "First in peace, and first in war."

Where the white-sailed ships are go - ing, Sail - ing to the o - cean blue;
Long, a - mong the an - gels num - bered, They the he - ro - soul have kept.
How he sleeps be-neath the wil - lows, "First in peace, and first in war."

Where the white-sailed ships are go - ing, Sail - ing to the o - cean blue;
Long, a - mong the an - gels num - bered, They the he - ro - soul have kept.
How he sleeps be-neath the wil - lows, "First in peace, and first in war."

Hushed the sound of mirth and sing - ing, Si - lent, ev - 'ry one;
But the chil-dren's chil - dren love him, And his name re - vere;
Tell, while sweet a - dieus are swell - ing, Till you come a - gain,

Hushed the sound of mirth and sing - ing, Si - lent, ev - 'ry one;
But the chil-dren's chil - dren love him, And his name re - vere;
Tell, while sweet a - dieus are swell - ing, Till you come a - gain,

Hushed the sound of mirth and sing - ing, Si - lent ev - 'ry one;
But the chil-dren's chil - dren love him, And his name re - vere;
Tell, while sweet a - dieus are swell - ing, Till you come a - gain,

While the sol-emn bells are ring - ing By the tomb of Wash-ing-ton.
So, where wil-lows wave a - bove him, Sweet-ly, still, his knell you hear.
He with-in the hearts is dwell - ing, Of his lov-ing coun-try-men.

While the sol-emn bells are ring - ing By the tomb of Wash-ing-ton.
So, where wil-lows wave a - bove him, Sweet-ly, still his knell you hear.
He with-in the hearts is dwell - ing, Of his lov-ing coun-try-men.

While the sol-emn bells are ring - ing By the tomb of Wash-ing-ton.
So, where wil-lows wave a - bove him, Sweet-ly, still, his knell you hear.
He with-in the hearts is dwell - ing, Of his lov-ing coun-try-men.

Toll - ing and knell - ing With a sad, sweet sound;

Toll - ing and knell - ing With a sad, sweet sound;

Toll - ing and knell - ing With a sad, sweet sound;

O'er the wave the tones are swell - ing, By Mount Ver-non's sa - cred ground.

O'er the wave the tones are swell - ing, By Mount Ver-non's sa - cred ground.

INDEPENDENCE DAY.

Words by M. B. C. S.

ALFRED LEE.

Lively.

SOLO, DUET, OR CHORUS IN UNISON.

1. The year is full of days that mark Our coun-try's grow-ing fame, Since sail-ing o'er the
2. Our coun-try's an-nals gleam and burn, That tell her sto-ried age. To-day with lov-ing
3. And tho' with grand he-ro-ic names, Our hearts are full to-day, Not one a high-er
4. Bring gar-lands of the fair-est flow'rs; Wreathe high the arch-es green; Let glad-ness fill the

wa-ters dark, Our Fa-thers hith-er came. Yet from new fields of glo-rious war, We
hand we turn Her no-blest ear-ly page; No day in all our na-tion's life So
trib-ute claims, Than those who *led the way;* We hon-or that de-vot-ed band Of
fly-ing hours, And glo-ry gild the scene; Let all the air re-sound with mirth, And

turn our eyes a-way, And gaze thro' gath-'ring years, a-far, On Freedom's na-tal day.
grand as this shall be; When, fac-ing death, and pain, and strife, They wrote, "All men are free!"
tried and tru-est worth;—Charles Car-roll of the South-ern land, John Hancock of the North!
songs of hap-py cheer; And crown the na-tion's day of birth, The best of all the year.

CHORUS.

1ST AND 2D SOPRANO.

Ring a mer-ry peal of bells, While the roar of can-non swells; Fling the ban-ners to the

ALTO-TENOR.

Ring a mer-ry peal of bells, While the roar of can-non swells; Fling the ban-ners to the

TENOR AND BASS.

Ring a mer-ry peal of bells, While the roar of can-non swells; Fling the ban-ners to the morn-ing breeze, Float the stream-ers o'er the land and seas; Spread the red, and white, and blue,

morn-ing breeze, Float the stream-ers o'er the land and seas; Spread the red, and white, and blue,

morn-ing breeze, Float the stream-ers o'er the land and seas; Spread the red, and white, and blue,

All the hap-py na-tion through, Shouting with a voice of glee, boys, A song for In-de-pendence Day!

All the hap-py na-tion through, Shouting with a voice of glee, boys, A song for In-de-pendence Day!

All the hap-py na-tion through, Shouting with a voice of glee, boys, A song for In-de-pendence Day!

Mrs. Hemans.
Miss Browne.

Allegro.

1. The break - ing waves dashed high   On a stern and rock - bound coast,
2. Not as the con - qu'ror comes,   They, the true - heart - ed, came;
3. A - midst the storm they sang,   And the stars heard, and the sea;
4. What sought they thus a - far?   Bright jew - els of the mine?

And the woods a - gainst a storm - y sky   Their gi - ant branch - es tossed;
Not with the roll of the stir - ring drums, And the trumpet that sings of fame;
And the sound - ing aisles of the dim woods rang   To the an - them of the free.
The wealth of seas, the spoils of war? They sought a faith's pure shrine!

And the heav - y night hung dark, The hills and wa - ters o'er,
Not as the fly - ing come, In si - lence and in fear;—
The o - cean ea - gle soared From his nest by the white wave's foam,
Ay, call it ho - ly ground, The soil where first they trod!

And the heav - y night hung dark, . The hills and wa - ters o'er, . .
Not as the fly - ing come, . In si - lence and in fear;—
The o - cean ea - gle soared . From his nest by the white wave's foam,
Ay, call it ho - ly ground, The soil where first they trod! . .

And the heav - y night hung dark, . The hills and wa - ters o'er, . .
Not as the fly - ing come, . In si - lence and in fear;—
The o - cean ea - gle soared From his nest by the white wave's foam,
Ay, call it ho - ly ground, The soil where first they trod! . .

When a band of ex - iles moored their bark On a wild New Eng - land shore.
They shook the depths of the des - ert gloom With their hymns of loft - y cheer.
And the rock - ing pines of the for - est roared,—This was their wel - come home!
They have left un-stained what there they found, Free - dom to wor - ship God.

When a band of ex - iles moored their bark On the wild New Eng - land shore.
They shook the depths of the des - ert gloom With their hymns of loft - y cheer.
And the rock - ing pines of the for - est roared,—This was their wel - come home!
They have left un-stained what there they found, Free - dom to wor - ship God.

When a band of ex - iles moored their bark On the wild New Eng - land shore.
They shook the depths of the des - ert gloom With their hymns of loft - y cheer.
And the rock - ing pines of the for - est roared,—This was their wel - come home home!
They have left un-stained what there they found, Free - dom to wor - ship God.

Words by GEO. P. MORRIS.   Music adapted by F. H. BROWN.

NOTE.—The melody of this song was called the " Drum and Fife March," by the Provincial army, and was a great favorite of the American troops, especially as it was played by them at the Battle of Yorktown. As the publisher is desirous of rescuing from oblivion a spirit-stirring melody, once so familiar in the American camp, it is here given anew.

1. I love the pa - triot sa - ges, Who in the days of yore, .. In
2. I love the loft - y spir - it That im-pell'd our sires to rise .. And

com-bat met the foe - men, And drove them from our shore; .. Who
found 'a mighty na - tion Be - neath the west-ern skies; .. Im-

in the days of yore, .. In com-bat met the foe - men, And drove them from our
pell'd our sires to rise .. And found a might - y na - tion Be-neath the west-ern

shore. ... Who flung our ban - ner's star - ry field, In tri - umph to the breeze,
skies. ... No clime so bright and beau - ti - ful As that where sets the sun;

1ST AND 2D SOPRANO.

And spread broad maps of ci - ties where Once wav'd the for - est trees; And spread broad maps of
No land so fer - tile, fair, and free, As that of Washing - ton; No land so fer - tile,

ALTO-TENOR.

And spread broad maps of ci - ties where Once wav'd the for - est trees; And spread broad maps of
No land so fer - tile, fair, and free, As that of Wash - ing - ton; No land so fer - tile,

TENOR AND BASS.

And spread broad maps of ci - ties where Once wav'd the for - est trees; And spread broad maps of
No land so fer - tile, fair, and free, As that of Wash - ing - ton; No land so fer - tile,

f

ci - ties where Once wav'd the for - est trees. Hur - rah! Hur - rah! Hur - rah! Hur - rah!
fair, and free, As that of Wash-ing - ton. Hur - rah! Hur - rah! Hur - rah! Hur - rah!

ci - ties where Once wav'd the for - est trees. Hur - rah! Hur - rah! Hur - rah! Hur - rah!
fair, and free, As that of Wash-ing - ton. Hur - rah! Hur - rah! Hur - rah! Hur - rah!

ci - ties where Once wav'd the for - est trees. Hur - rah! Hur - rah! Hur - rah! Hur - rah!
fair, and free, As that of Wash-ing - ton. Hur - rah! Hur - rah! Hur - rah! Hur - rah!

ff

ODE FOR WASHINGTON'S BIRTHDAY.

Oliver Wendell Holmes (1809–1894).

Ludwig van Beethoven (1770–1827).
(From the Ninth or Choral Symphony.)

1st and 2d Soprano.

1. Wel - come to the day re - turn - ing, Dear - er still as a - ges flow,
2. Hear the tale of youth - ful glo - ry, While of Brit - ain's res - cued band;
3. Look! the shad - ow on the di - al Marks the hour of dead - lier strife;
4. Vain is Em - pire's mad temp - ta - tion! Not for him an earth - ly crown!
5. "By the name that you in - her - it, By the suf - f'rings you re - call,
6. "Fa - ther! we whose ears have tin - gled With the dis - cord notes of shame,—

Alto-Tenor.

1. Wel - come to the day re - turn - ing, Dear - er still as a - ges flow,
2. Hear the tale of youth - ful glo - ry, While of Brit - ain's res - cued band;
3. Look! the shad - ow on the di - al Marks the hour of dead - lier strife;
4. Vain is Em - pire's mad temp - ta - tion! Not for him an earth - ly crown!
5. "By the name that you in - her - it, By the suf - f'rings you re - call,
6. "Fa - ther! we whose ears have tin - gled With the dis - cord notes of shame,—

Tenor and Bass.

While the torch of faith is burn - ing, Long as free - dom's al - tars glow!
Friend and foe re - peat the sto - ry, Spread his fame o'er sea and land,
Days of ter - ror, years of tri - al, Scourge a na - tion in - to life.
He, whose sword has freed a na - tion, Strikes the of - fered scep - tre down.
Cher - ish the fra - ter - nal spir - it; Love your coun - try first of all!
We, whose sires their blood have min - gled In the bat - tle's thun - der flame,—

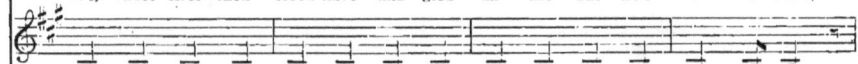

While the torch of faith is burn - ing, Long as free - dom's al - tars glow!
Friend and foe re - peat the sto - ry, Spread his fame o'er sea and land,
Days of ter - ror, years of tri - al, Scourge a na - tion in - to life.
He, whose sword has freed a na - tion, Strikes the of - fered scep - tre down.
Cher - ish the fra - ter - nal spir - it; Love your coun - try first of all!
We, whose sires their blood have min - gled In the bat - tle's thun - der flame,—

Used by special permission of Houghton, Mifflin & Co., Publishers.

See the he - ro whom it gave us Slum - b'ring on a moth - er's breast;
Where the red cross, fond - ly stream - ing, Flaps a - bove the frig - ate's deck;
Lo, the youth, be - come her lead - er! All her baf - fled ty - rants yield;
See the throne - less con - queror seat - ed, Rul - er by a peo - ple's choice;
List - en not to i - dle ques - tions If its bands may be un - tied;
Gath -'ring while this ho - ly morn - ing Lights the land from sea to sea,

See the he - ro whom it gave us Slum - b'ring on a moth - er's breast;
Where the red cross, fond - ly stream - ing, Flaps a - bove the frig - ate's deck;
Lo, the youth, be - come her lead - er! All her baf - fled ty - rants yield;
See the throne - less con - queror seat - ed, Rul - er by a peo - ple's choice;
List - en not to i - dle ques - tions If its bands may be un - tied;
Gath -'ring while this ho - ly morn - ing Lights the land from sea to sea,

For the arm he stretched to save us, Be its morn for ev - er blest.
Where the gold - en lil - ies, gleam - ing, Star the watch-tow'rs of Que - bec.
Through his arm the Lord hath freed her; Crown him on the tent - ed field!
See the Pa - triot's task com - plet - ed; Hear the Fa - ther's dy - ing voice:
Doubt the pa - triot whose sug - ges - tions Strive a na - tion to di - vide!"
Hear thy coun - sel, heed thy warn - ing; Trust us, while we hon - or thee!

For the arm he stretched to save us, Be its morn for ev - er blest.
Where the gold - en lil - ies, gleam - ing, Star the watch-tow'rs of Que - bec.
Through his arm the Lord hath freed her; Crown him on the tent - ed field!
See the Pa - triot's task com - plet - ed; Hear the Fa - ther's dy - ing voice:
Doubt the pa - triot whose sug - ges - tions Strive a na - tion to di - vide!"
Hear thy coun - sel, heed thy warn - ing; Trust us, while we hon - or thee!

SONG OF COLUMBUS DAY.

Theron Brown.

Franz Joseph Haydn (1732–1809).

1st and 2d Soprano.

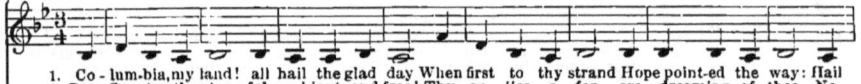

1. Co-lum-bia, my land! all hail the glad day When first to thy strand Hope point-ed the way: Hail
2. Dear Country, the star of the val-iant and free! Thy ex - iles a - far are dreaming of thee, No
3. Thy fair-est es -tate the low - ly may hold, Thy poor may grow great, thy fee - ble grow bold: For
4. O Un-ion of States, and un - ion of souls! Thy prom-ise a-waits, thy fu - ture un - folds, And

Alto-Tenor.

1. Co-lum-bia, my land! all hail the glad day When first to thy strand Hope point-ed the way: Hail
2. Dear Country, the star of the val-iant and free! Thy ex - iles a - far are dreaming of thee, No
3. Thy fair-est es - tate the low - ly may hold, Thy poor may grow great, thy fee - ble grow bold: For
4. O Un-ion of States, and un - ion of souls! Thy prom-ise a-waits, thy fu - ture un - folds, And

Tenor and Bass.

1. Co-lum-bia, my land! all hail the glad day When first to thy strand Hope point-ed the way: Hail
2. Dear Conntry, the star of the val-iant and free! Thy ex - iles a - far are dreaming of thee, No
3. Thy fair-est es- tate the low - ly may hold, Thy poor may grow great, thy fee - ble grow bold: For
4. O Un-ion of States, and un - ion of souls! Thy prom-ise a-waits, thy fu - ture un - folds, And

him who thro' darkness first followed the Flame That led where the Mayflow'r of Lib - er - ty came.
fields of the earth so en-chanting - ly shine, No air breathes such incense, such mu - sic as thine.
worth is the watchword to no - ble de-gree, And man-hood is might-y where man-hood is free.
earth from her twi-light is hail-ing the sun, That ris - es where peo-ple and ru - lers are one.

him who thro' darkness first followed the Flame That led where the Mayflow'r of Lib - er - ty came.
fields of the earth so en-chanting - ly shine, No air breathes such incense, such mu - sic as thine.
worth is the watchword to no - ble de-gree, And man-hood is might-y where man-hood is free.
earth from her twi-light is hail-ing the sun, That ris - es where peo-ple and ru - lers are one.

him who thro' darkness first followed the Flame That led where the Mayflow'r of Lib - er - ty came.
fields of the earth so en-chanting - ly shine, No air breathes such incense, such mu - sic as thine.
worth is the watchword to no - ble de-gree, And man-hood is might-y where man-hood is free.
earth from her twi-light is hail-ing the sun, That ris - es where peo-ple and ru - lers are one.

MISCELLANEOUS

GOD OF THE NATIONS.

ANVIL CHORUS, FROM "IL TROVATORE."

G. VERDI.

God of the na-tions, in glo-ry en-thron-ed, Up-on our lov'd coun-try Thy bless-ings pour; Guide us and guard us from strife in the fu-ture, Let Peace dwell a-mong us for ev - er - more!

Proud - ly our ban - ner now gleams with gold - en lus - tre! Bright - er each star . . shines in the glo - rious clus - ter! Lib - er - ty for ev - er - more! And Peace and Un - ion, And Peace and Un - ion throughout our hap - py land. land.

A PATRIOTIC PART-SONG.

Words by Geo. Cooper.
Molto animato.

Music by Brinley Richards.

land, . Ev-er free Co-lum-bia stand! And this our mot-to be while we march a-

land, . Ev-er free Co-lum-bia stand! And this our mot-to be while we march a-

land, . Ev-er free Co-lum-bia stand! And this our mot-to be while we march a-

long.   Sires . of old, . your fame is writ in gold, . Your her-i-tage we

long. .   Sires . of old, . your fame is writ in gold, . Your her-i-tage we

long. .   Sires . of old, . your fame is writ in gold, . Your her-i-tage we

treas-ure and your man-dates heed. . While Time . shall last, . No stain shall e'er be

treas-ure and your man-dates heed. . While Time . shall last, . No stain shall e'er be

treas-ure and your man-dates heed. . While Time . shall last, . No stain shall e'er be

Let the
cast . To dim the light that shines a-bove each pa-triot deed. The
cast . To dim the light that shines a-bove each pa-triot deed. The
cast . To dim the light that shines a-bove each pa-triot deed. The
hills and vales re-sound, Ev-'ry heart with rap-ture bound! Our flag doth fly 'neath
hills and vales re-sound, Ev-'ry heart with rap-ture bound! Our flag doth fly 'neath
hills and vales re-sound, Ev-'ry heart with rap-ture bound! Our flag doth fly 'neath
Free-dom's sky, Wake now our song! Oh, bless our na-tive land, Ev-er free Co-lum-bia
Free-dom's sky, Wake now our song! Oh, bless our na-tive land, Ev-er free Co-lum-bia
Free-dom's sky, Wake now our song! Oh, bless our na-tive land, Ev-er free Co-lum-bia

stand! And this our mot - to be While we march a - long.

stand! And this our mot - to be While we march a - long. Na - tive land, dear

stand! And this our mot - to be While we march a - long. Na - tive land, dear

Dear na - tive land, 'Neath thy stars we stand, Ev - 'ry heart for - ev - er thy shield will be. As in

na - tive land, dear land of home, Our hearts for - e'er thy shield will be. As in

home, Be - neath thy stars we stand, Our hearts for - e'er thy shield will be. As in

home, Be - neath thy stars we stand, Our hearts for - e'er thy shield will be. As in

days of old, When first un - rolled, Flag of our na - tion, we march 'neath thee.

days of old, When first un - rolled, Flag of our na - tion, we march 'neath thee.

days of old, When first un - rolled, Flag of our na - tion, we march 'neath thee.

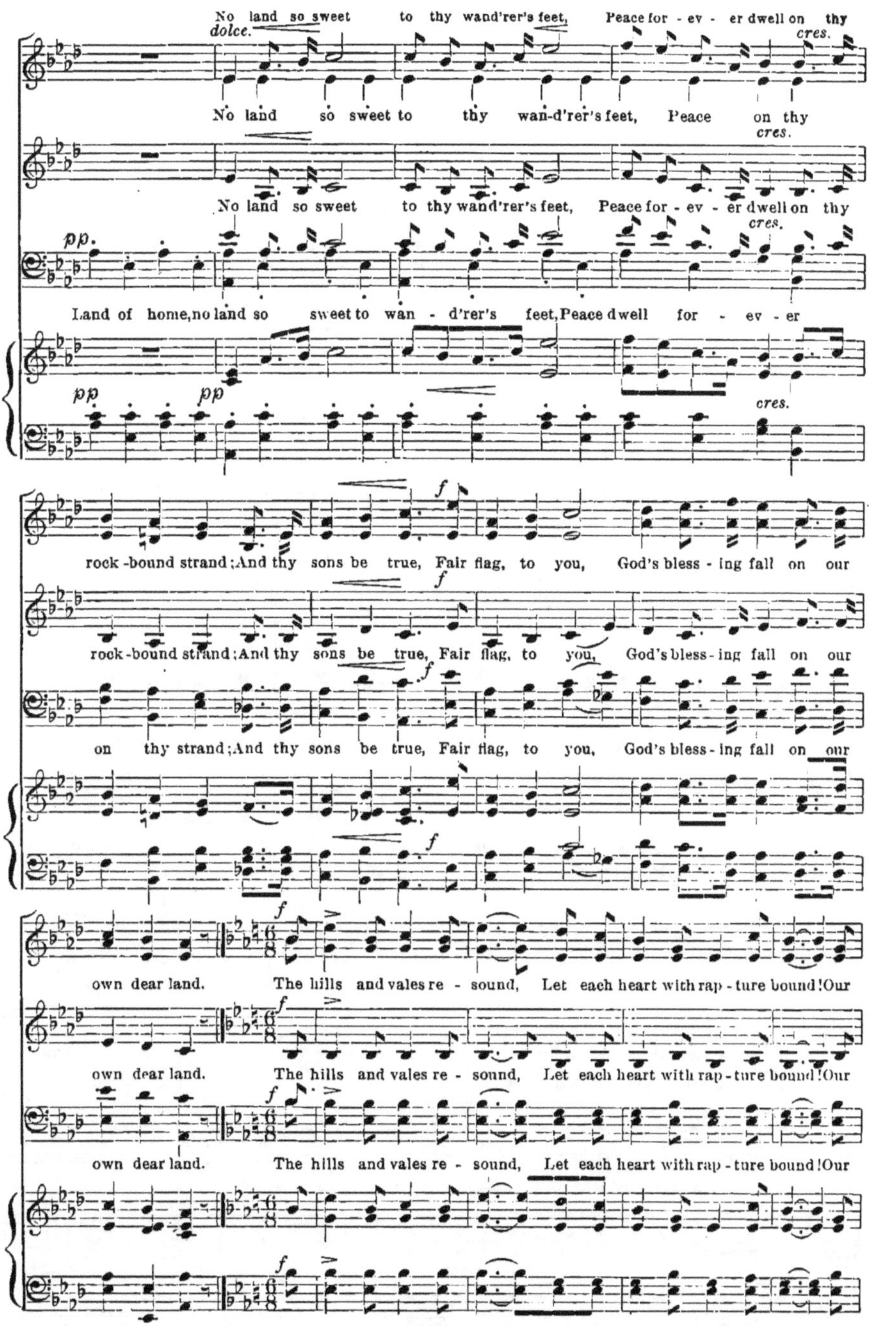

flag doth fly 'neath Freedom's sky, Wake now our song! Oh, bless our na - tive land, Ev - er

flag doth fly 'neath Freedom's sky, Wake now our song! Oh, bless our na - tive land, Ev - er

flag doth fly 'neath Freedom's sky, Wake now our song! Oh, bless our na - tive land, Ev - er

free Co - lum - bia stand! And this our mot - to be while we march a - long, The

free Co - lum - bia stand! And this our mot - to be while we march a - long, The hills, the

free Co - lum - bia stand! And this our mot - to be while we march a - long, The hills, the

hills and vales re - sound, re-sound with song, re - sound with song.

hills and vales resound with song, re-sound with song, re - sound with song.

hills and vales resound with song, re-sound with song, re - sound with song.

LOYAL SONG.

C. J. Sprague.
1st and 2d Soprano.

Friedrich W. Kücken. (1810–1882.)
Arranged by F. A. W.

Allegro con moto.

Free-dom dwells throughout our own be - lov - ed land: Up to Heav'n its voice is

Alto - Tenor.

Free-dom dwells throughout our own be - lov - ed land: Up to Heav'n its voice is

Tenor and Bass.

Free-dom dwells throughout our own be - lov - ed land: Up to Heav'n its voice is

swell - ing, From the mountain heights a - far to o - cean strand, Ev - 'ry breeze the tale is

swell - ing, From the mountain heights a - far to o - cean strand, Ev - 'ry breeze the tale is

swell - ing, From the mountain heights a - far to o - cean strand, Ev - 'ry breeze the tale is tell - ing. Nev - er wea - ry of the ev - er joy - ous song, Heart and voice u -

tell - ing. Nev - er wea - ry of the ev - er joy - ous song, Heart and voice u -

tell - ing. The ev - er joy - ous song, Heart and voice u -

nit - ed bear a - long, Loy - al to the end! Read - y to de - fend!

nit - ed bear a - long, Loy - al to the end! Read - y to de - fend!

nit - ed bear a - long, Loy - al to the end! Read - y to de - fend!

Foe with - in and out re - pell - ing, Foe with - in and out re -

Foe with - in and out re - pell - ing, Foe with -

Foe with - in and out re - pell - ing, Foe with -

cres.
pell - ing, Loy - al to the end! Ready - y to de - fend!
in and out re - pell - ing, Loy - al to the end! Read - y to de - fend!
in and out re - pell - ing, Loy - al to the end! to the end! Read - y to de - fend! to defend!
ff
Loy - al to the end! Loy - al to the end! Foe with-in and out re -
Loy - al to the end! Loy - al to the end! Foe with-in and out re -
sfz
pell - ing, All loy - al to the end! Foe with-in and out re - pell - ing.
pell - ing, All loy - al to the end! Foe with-in and out re - pell - ing.
pell - ing, All loy - al to the end! Foe with-in and out re - pell - ing.

MARCH OF THE MEN OF COLUMBIA.

Words by H. A. CLARKE.

Welsh air, "March of the Men of Harlech."
Harmonized by JOSEPH BARNBY.

1. From the hill - side, from the hol - low, Do you hear like rush - ing bil - low,
2. Lo, the ty - rant's days are num-bered, Lib - er - ty no long - er slum - bers,

1. From the hill - side, from the hol - low, Do you hear like rush - ing bil - low,
2. Lo, the ty - rant's days are num-bered, Lib - er - ty no long - er slum - bers,

1. From the hill - side, from the hol - low, Do you hear like rush - ing bil - low,
2. Lo, the ty - rant's days are num-bered, Lib - er - ty no long - er slum - bers,

Wave on wave, that surg - ing fol - low, Till they shake the ground. Hail this day of hap - py o - men,
Er - ror dark no long - er cum-bers, Ris - en is the sun. North and south, fell hate de - fy - ing,

Wave on wave, that surg - ing fol - low, Till they shake the ground. Hail this day of hap - py o - men,
Er - ror dark no long - er cum-bers, Ris - en is the sun. North and south, fell hate de - fy - ing,

Wave on wave, that surg - ing fol - low, Till they shake the ground. Hail this day of hap - py o - men,
Er - ror dark no long - er cum-bers, Ris - en is the sun. North and south, fell hate de - fy - ing,

'Tis the tramp of gath-'ring free-men, La - bor's hosts of stur - dy yeo - men, Swell th'ex-ult - ing
East and west, with love un - dy - ing, All in friend-ship true are vie - ing, Firm - ly bound in

'Tis the tramp of gath-'ring free-men, La - bor's hosts of stur - dy yeo - men, Swell th'ex-ult - ing
East and west, with love un - dy - ing, All in friend-ship true are vie - ing, Firm - ly bound in

'Tis the tramp of gath-'ring free-men, La - bor's hosts of stur - dy yeo - men, Swell th'ex-ult - ing
East and west, with love un - dy - ing, All in friend-ship true are vie - ing, Firm - ly bound in

sound. Loose the folds a - sun - der, Flag we ral - ly un - der; The pla - cid sky, now
one. Loud - er swell the cho - rus, Till the wel - kin o'er us Re - flects a - gain the

sound. Loose the folds a - sun - der, Flag we ral - ly un - der; The pla - cid sky, now
one. Loud - er swell the cho - rus, Till the wel - kin o'er us Re - flects a - gain the

sound. Loose the folds a - sun - der, Flag we ral - ly un - der; The pla - cid sky, now
one. Loud - er swell the cho - rus, Till the wel - kin o'er us Re - flects a - gain the

bright on high, We'll rend with shouts like thun-der. On-ward press, our coun-try needs us;
joy - ous strain, And dis - cord flies be - fore us. On-ward press, our coun-try needs us;

bright on high, We'll rend with shouts like thun-der. On-ward press, our coun-try needs us;
joy - ous strain, And dis - cord flies be - fore us. On-ward press, our coun-try needs us;

bright on high, We'll rend with shouts like thun-der. On-ward press, our coun-try needs us;
joy - ous strain, And dis - cord flies be - fore us. On-ward press, our coun-try needs us;

On - ward press, 'tis glo - ry leads us; Hark! the watchword high that speeds us, Freedom, God, and Right.

On - ward press, 'tis glo - ry leads us; Hark! the watchword high that speeds us, Freedom, God, and Right.

On - ward press, 'tis glo - ry leads us; Hark! the watchword high that speeds us, Freedom, God, and Right.

O LAND BELOVED!

J. C. Macy.

Carl Wilhelm (1815-1875.)
Air: "Die Wacht am Rhein."

Maestoso.

1st and 2d Soprano

1. O land be-lov'd, O bright, free land, Re-ceive our gifts of heart and hand; Our
2. Where ride our ships whose guns are mann'd By sea-men brave—a daunt-less band,—Or
3. Then guard it well, this home we love; Keep Free-dom's light un-dimm'd a-bove; Pre-

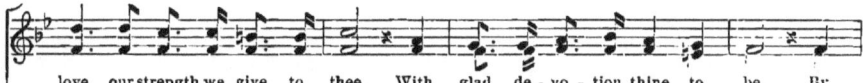

Alto-Tenor.

1. O land be-lov'd, O bright, free land, Re-ceive our gifts of heart and hand; Our
2. Where ride our ships whose guns are mann'd By sea-men brave— a daunt-less band,—Or
3. Then guard it well, this home we love; Keep Free-dom's light un-dimm'd a-bove; Pre-

Tenor and Bass.

1. O land be-lov'd, O bright, free land, Re-ceive our gifts of heart and hand; Our
2. Where ride our ships whose guns are mann'd By sea-men brave— a daunt-less band,—Or
3. Then guard it well, this home we love; Keep Free-dom's light un-dimm'd a-bove; Pre-

love, our strength we give to thee, With glad de-vo-tion thine to be. By
where our ar-my, con-q'ring still, Spreads grand-ly o-ver vale and hill— There
serve with care and rev-'rent hand A-mer-i-ca, the heav'n-blest land! The

love, our strength we give to thee, With glad de-vo-tion thine to be. By
where our ar-my, con-q'ring still, Spreads grand-ly o-ver vale and hill— There
serve with care and rev-'rent hand A-mer-i-ca, the heav'n-blest land! The

love, our strength we give to thee, With glad de-vo-tion thine to be. By
where our ar-my, con-q'ring still, Spreads grand-ly o-ver vale and hill— There
serve with care and rev-'rent hand A-mer-i-ca, the heav'n-blest land! The

blood of pa-triots thou wast won; Thy truths pass'd on from sire to son. Blest land! Our
earth and sea, 'neath heav-en's light, Seem glad to hail the no - ble sight! Blest land! Our
stars and stripes, our flag for aye! This grand, free coun-try, ours to - day! Blest land! Our

blood of pa-triots thou wast won; Thy truths pass'd on from sire to son. Blest land! Our
earth and sea, 'neath heav-en's light, Seem glad to hail the no - ble sight! Blest land! Our
stars and stripes, our flag for aye! This grand, free coun-try, ours to - day! Blest land! Our

blood of pa-triots thou wast won; Thy truths pass'd on from sire to son. Blest land! Our
earth and sea, 'neath heav-en's light, Seem glad to hail the no - ble sight! Blest land! Our
stars and stripes, our flag for aye! This grand, free coun-try, ours to - day! Blest land! Our

home be-lov'd! O Free-dom's land! True to thy flag to-day Thy chil-dren stand.

home be-lov'd! O Free-dom's land! True to thy flag to-day Thy chil-dren stand.

home be-lov'd! O Free-dom's land! True to thy flag to-day Thy chil-dren stand.

TENTING ON THE OLD CAMP GROUND.

Arranged by F.

Words and Music by WALTER KITTREDGE.

Tempo di Marcia.

1. We're tent - ing to-night on the old Camp ground,
2. We've been tent - ing to - night on the old Camp ground,
3. We are tir - ed of war on the old Camp ground,
4. We've been fight - ing to - day on the old Camp ground,

Give us a song to cheer Our wea - ry hearts, a
Think-ing of days gone by, Of the lov'd ones at home that
Man - y are dead and gone, Of the brave and true who've
Man - y are ly - ing near; Some are dead, and

song of . . home And friends we love so dear.
gave us the hand, And the tear that said "Good - bye!"
left their homes, Oth - ers been wound - ed long.
some are dy - ing, . Man - y are in tears.

CHORUS.

1ST AND 2D SOPRANO.

Man - y are the hearts that are wea - ry to - night, Wish-ing for the war to

ALTO-TENOR.

Man - y are the hearts that are wea - ry to - night, Wish-ing for the war to

TENOR AND BASS.

Man - y are the hearts that are wea - ry to - night, Wish-ing for the war to

cease;   Man - y are the hearts that are look-ing for the right   To

cease;   Man - y are the hearts that are look-ing for the right   To

cease;   Man - y are the hearts that are look-ing for the right   To

see the dawn of peace. Tent-ing to-night, Tent-ing to-night,
Last verse Dy-ing to-night, Dy-ing to-night,

see the dawn of peace. Tent-ing to-night, Tent-ing to-night,
Last verse Dy-ing to-night, Dy-ing to-night,

see the dawn of peace. Tent-ing to-night, Tent-ing to-night,
Last verse Dy-ing to-night, Dy-ing to-night,

Last verse.
ppp molto rit.

Tent-ing on the old Camp ground. Dy-ing on the old Camp ground.

Tent-ing on the old Camp ground. Dy-ing on the old Camp ground.

Tent-ing on the old Camp ground. Dy-ing on the old Camp ground.

Last verse.

pp molto rit. *ppp*

THE SOLDIER'S FAREWELL.

Translated from the German by Louis C. Elson.   Johanna Kinkel (1810-1858).

Andante.

1st and 2d Soprano.

1. How can I bear to leave thee?One part-ing kiss I give thee; And then,whate'er be - falls me, I
2. Ne'er more may I be-hold thee, Or to this heart en-fold thee;With spear and pen-non glanc-ing, I
3. I think of thee with long-ing;Think thou,when tears are thronging,That with my last faint sighing, I'll

Alto-Tenor.

1. How can I bear to leave thee?One part-ing kiss I give thee; And then,whate'er be - falls me, I
2. Ne'er more may I be-hold thee, Or to this heart en-fold thee;With spear and pen-non glanc-ing, I
3. I think of thee with long-ing;Think thou,when tears are thronging,That with my last faint sighing, I'll

Tenor and Bass.

1. How can I bear to leave thee?One part-ing kiss I give thee; And then,whate'er be - falls me, I
2. Ne'er more may I be-hold thee, Or to this heart en-fold thee;With spear and pen-non glanc-ing, I
3. I think of thee with long-ing;Think thou,when tears are thronging,That with my last faint sighing, I'll

Tempo 1. tranquillo e molto espress.

go where hon-or calls me. Fare - well,fare-well, my own true love,Farewell,fare-well, my own true love.
see the foe ad - vanc-ing. Fare - well,fare-well, my own true love,Farewell,fare-well, my own true love.
whisper soft,while dy - ing, Fare - well,fare-well, my own true love,Farewell,fare-well, my own true love.

go where hon-or calls me. Fare - well,fare-well, my own true love,Farewell,fare-well, my own true love.
see the foe ad - vanc-ing. Fare - well,fare-well, my own true love,Farewell,fare-well, my own true love.
whisper soft,while dy - ing, Fare - well,fare-well, my own true love,Farewell,fare-well, my own true love.

go where hon-or calls me. Fare - well,fare-well, my own true love,Farewell,fare-well, my own true love.
see the foe ad - vanc-ing. Fare - well,fare-well, my own true love,Farewell,fare-well, my own true love.
whisper soft,while dy - ing, Fare - well,fare-well, my own true love,Farewell,fare-well, my own true love.

Tempo 1.

p tranquillo e molto espress.

YANKEE DOODLE.

Air unknown. Arr. by F. C.

Origin of Yankee Doodle.—The tune, which originated in France or Holland, was first sung in England to the nursery rhyme "Lucy Locket Lost her Pocket." It was soon adapted to verses sung by the Cavaliers in ridicule of Cromwell, who was said to have entered Oxford riding a small horse and wearing a single plume fastened to a knot called in derision a "macaroni." In the summer of 1755, the British army lay encamped on the east bank of the Hudson river near Albany, awaiting reinforcements of militia from the Eastern Colonies previous to marching on Ticonderoga. During the month of June these raw levies poured into camp, company after company, each man differently armed and equipped from his neighbors, and the motley whole presenting a spectacle that greatly amused the British officers. Dr. Shamburg, a joke-loving surgeon, gave the new recruits this song, gravely dedicating it to them. To the great amusement of the British the joke took. Twenty-six years later Cornwallis marched to the same tune into the lines of these same old Continentals to surrender his sword and his army.

With spirit.

1. Fa - ther and I went down to camp, A - long with Cap-tain Good - win, And
2. And there was Cap - tain Wash-ing - ton Up - on a slap-ping stal - lion, And
3. And then the feath - ers on his hat, They looked so tar - nal fi - ney, I
4. And there they had a swamp-ing gun, As big as a log of ma - ple,

there we saw the men and boys, As thick as has - ty pud - ding.
giv - ing or - ders to his men; I guess there was a mil - lion.
want - ed pesk - i - ly to get To give to my Je - mi - ma.
On a deuc - ed lit - tle cart,—A load for fa - ther's cat - tle.

YANKEE DOODLE.

CHORUS.
1ST AND 2D SOPRANO.

Yan - kee Doo - dle, keep it up, Yan - kee Doo - dle dan - dy,

ALTO—TENOR.

Yan - kee Doo - dle, keep it up. Yan - kee Doo - dle dan - dy,

TENOR AND BASS.

Yan - kee Doo - dle, keep it up, Yan - kee Doo - dle dan - dy,

Mind the mu - sic and the step, And with the girls be hand - y.

Mind the mu - sic and the step, And with the girls be hand - y.

Mind the mu - sic and the step, And with the girls be hand - y.

5 And every time they fired it off
   It took a horn of powder;
   It made a noise like father's gun,
   Only a nation louder.

6 I went as near to it myself,
   As Jacob's underpinin';
   And father went as near again —
   I thought the deuce was in him.

7 (It scared me so, I ran the streets,
   Nor stopped as I remember,
   Till I got home, and safely locked
   In granny's little chamber.)

8 And there I see a little keg;
   Its heads were made of leather.
   They knock   with little sticks,
   To call the   ther.

9 And there they'd fife away like fun,
   And play on corn-stalk fiddles;
   And some had ribbons red as blood,
   All bound around their middles.

10 The troopers too, would gallop up,
   And fire right in our faces;
   It scared me almost half to death,
   To see them run such races.

11 Uncle Sam came there to change
   Some pancakes and some onions
   For 'lasses cakes to carry home
   To give his wife and young ones.

12 But I can't tell you half I see,
   They keep up such a smother,
   So I took my hat off, made a bow,
   And scampered home to mother.

INDEX.

www.ingramcontent.com/pod-product-compliance
Lightning Source LLC
Chambersburg PA
CBHW030833270326
41928CB00007B/1035